"The Bible is essential for Christian spirituality. Central to the Bible are the teachings of Jesus. Among those teachings, none are more fundamental than the Sermon on the Mount. *A Fruitful Life*, by Ashley and Bryce Hales, digs deeply into these famous and powerful words, providing readers fresh insights for growing as followers of Jesus. I highly recommend it for church groups of all kinds."

Todd Hunter, author of *What Jesus Intended*

"The twenty-first century brims with peace and prosperity and technology the likes of which no generation has ever known. And yet many people feel dead inside. Maybe you are exhausted by the 'survival of the fittest' culture all around you and the numbness it leaves behind. If so, read this book. Ashley and Bryce Hales reintroduce us to Jesus' Sermon on the Mount, peeling through the familiarity of it to get at the shocking, joyous, life-upending power of it."

Russell Moore, editor in chief of Christianity Today

"I am always looking for studies to recommend to small groups—studies that invite people into deeper community and individual time with God or devotionals that are diligent in engaging with the Scriptures and commend ways for us to practice our faith. In *A Fruitful Life*, Ashley and Bryce Hales give us just such a resource: an exploration of Jesus' Sermon on the Mount that is both invitational and challenging for Christians at any stage of their spiritual journey to live more fruitfully."

Bronwyn Lea, pastor and author of *Beyond Awkward Side Hugs*

"This is a refreshing and illuminating study, drawing out the meaning and significance of the Sermon on the Mount for Jesus followers today. Ashley and Bryce Hales guide readers through Jesus' words with care and conviction. This study is a gift to the church."

Kaitlyn Schiess, author of *The Ballot and the Bible* and *The Liturgy of Politics*

"The Christian life isn't lived in abstraction. As much as ethical codes, theological principles, and worldviews can be helpful in comprehending our faith, we actually follow Jesus in the gritty reality of day-to-day life—getting ready for school, dealing with tension in the workplace, suffering the frailty of the body, and stretching our budgets to make ends meet. Thankfully, while Christians are often drawn to abstraction, Jesus' teaching has a way of calling us back to the concrete, challenging us with a way of seeing, living, and praying that avoids escapism and roots us in love of God and neighbor. This is good news, and it's the central truth behind this marvelous work by Ashley and Bryce Hales. They invite us to consider Jesus' words in the soil of the everyday, helping us to reconsider the familiar and see our neighbors, friends, and everyday lives in the light of the Sermon on the Mount. It's a refreshing perspective in a moment when the church, now as ever, needs to reimagine what it means to follow Jesus in polarizing times."

Mike Cosper, director of podcasts for Christianity Today and author of *Land of My Sojourn*

"I can think of no portion of the Bible that calls for a companion guide more than Jesus' Sermon on the Mount. There are simply too many treasures to unearth to move through it quickly or haphazardly. What a gift, then, that Ashley and Bryce Hales have put together such a marvelous study guide for this most world- and life-changing of passages. Full of fresh insight, genuine usefulness, and a palpable love for the one who preached, *A Fruitful Life* will undoubtedly bear abundant fruit itself."

David Zahl, director of Mockingbird Ministries and author of *Low Anthropology*

A FRUITFUL LIFE

ASHLEY HALES & BRYCE HALES

An imprint of InterVarsity Press
Downers Grove, Illinois

InterVarsity Press
P.O. Box 1400 | Downers Grove, IL 60515-1426
ivpress.com | email@ivpress.com

InterVarsity Press® is the publishing division of InterVarsity Christian Fellowship/USA®. For more information, visit intervarsity.org.

Published in association with the literary agent Don Gates of The Gates Group, www.the-gates-group.com.

Art by Ned Bustard, www.worldsendimages.com. Used by permission.

The Return of the Prodigal Son, Rembrandt, circa 1668, courtesy Wikimedia Commons.

Interior images: iStock / Getty Images Plus: ©kevinhillillustration, ©VectorGoods, ©Iryna Haiovyk; DigitalVision Vectors: ©DivVectors, ©johnwoodcock; ©CSA Images / CSA Images

Cover design: Faceout Studio
Interior design: Jeanna Wiggins

ISBN 978-1-5140-0718-1 (print) | ISBN 978-1-5140-0719-8 (digital)

Printed in the United States of America ♾

Library of Congress Cataloging-in-Publication Data
Names: Hales, Ashley, 1980 – author. | Hales, Bryce, 1980 – author.
Title: A fruitful life: discovering Jesus' invitation in the Sermon on the mount: an 8-week Bible study / Ashley Hales and Bryce Hales.
Description: Downers Grove, IL: InterVarsity Press, [2025] | Series: IVP Bible studies
Identifiers: LCCN 2024042533 (print) | LCCN 2024042534 (ebook) | ISBN 9781514007181 (paperback) | ISBN 9781514007198 (ebook)
Subjects: LCSH: Sermon on the mount--Study and teaching. | Bible. Matthew, V-VII--Criticism, interpretation, etc. | Spiritual formation--Biblical teaching. | Christian life--Biblical teaching.
Classification: LCC BT380.3 .H35 2025 (print) | LCC BT380.3 (ebook) | DDC 226.907–dc23/eng/20241025
LC record available at https://lccn.loc.gov/2024042533
LC ebook record available at https://lccn.loc.gov/2024042534

30 29 28 27 26 25 | 8 7 6 5 4 3 2 1

CONTENTS

MATTHEW 5–7

THE SERMON ON THE MOUNT

5 Seeing the crowds, he went up on the
mountain, and when he sat down, his
disciples came to him.
2 And he opened his mouth and taught
them, saying:
3 "Blessed are the poor in spirit, for theirs is
the kingdom of heaven.
4 "Blessed are those who mourn, for they
shall be comforted.
5 "Blessed are the meek, for they shall inherit the earth.
6 "Blessed are those who hunger and thirst
for righteousness, for they shall be satisfied.
7 "Blessed are the merciful, for they shall
receive mercy.
8 "Blessed are the pure in heart, for they
shall see God.
9 "Blessed are the peacemakers, for they
shall be called sons of God.
10 "Blessed are those who are persecuted for
righteousness' sake, for theirs is the kingdom
of heaven.
11 "Blessed are you when others revile you and
persecute you and utter all kinds of evil against
you falsely on my account. 12 Rejoice and be glad,
for your reward is great in heaven, for so they
persecuted the prophets who were before you.
13 "You are the salt of the earth, but if salt has
lost its taste, how shall its saltiness be restored?
It is no longer good for anything except to be
thrown out and trampled under people's feet.
14 "You are the light of the world. A city set
on a hill cannot be hidden. 15 Nor do people
light a lamp and put it under a basket, but on
a stand, and it gives light to all in the house.
16 In the same way, let your light shine before
others, so that they may see your good works
and give glory to your Father who is in heaven.
17 "Do not think that I have come to abolish
the Law or the Prophets; I have not come to
abolish them but to fulfill them. 18 For truly, I
say to you, until heaven and earth pass away,
not an iota, not a dot, will pass from the Law
until all is accomplished. 19 Therefore whoever
relaxes one of the least of these commandments and teaches others to do the same will
be called least in the kingdom of heaven, but
whoever does them and teaches them will be
called great in the kingdom of heaven. 20 For I
tell you, unless your righteousness exceeds

that of the scribes and Pharisees, you will never enter the kingdom of heaven.

[21] "You have heard that it was said to those of old, 'You shall not murder; and whoever murders will be liable to judgment.' [22] But I say to you that everyone who is angry with his brother will be liable to judgment; whoever insults his brother will be liable to the council; and whoever says, 'You fool!' will be liable to the hell of fire. [23] So if you are offering your gift at the altar and there remember that your brother has something against you, [24] leave your gift there before the altar and go. First be reconciled to your brother, and then come and offer your gift. [25] Come to terms quickly with your accuser while you are going with him to court, lest your accuser hand you over to the judge, and the judge to the guard, and you be put in prison. [26] Truly, I say to you, you will never get out until you have paid the last penny.

[27] "You have heard that it was said, 'You shall not commit adultery.' [28] But I say to you that everyone who looks at a woman with lustful intent has already committed adultery with her in his heart. [29] If your right eye causes you to sin, tear it out and throw it away. For it is better that you lose one of your members than that your whole body be thrown into hell. [30] And if your right hand causes you to sin, cut it off and throw it away. For it is better that you lose one of your members than that your whole body go into hell.

[31] "It was also said, 'Whoever divorces his wife, let him give her a certificate of divorce.' [32] But I say to you that everyone who divorces his wife, except on the ground of sexual immorality, makes her commit adultery, and whoever marries a divorced woman commits adultery.

[33] "Again you have heard that it was said to those of old, 'You shall not swear falsely, but shall perform to the Lord what you have sworn.' [34] But I say to you, Do not take an oath at all, either by heaven, for it is the throne of God, [35] or by the earth, for it is his footstool, or by Jerusalem, for it is the city of the great King. [36] And do not take an oath by your head, for you cannot make one hair white or black. [37] Let what you say be simply 'Yes' or 'No'; anything more than this comes from evil.

[38] "You have heard that it was said, 'An eye for an eye and a tooth for a tooth.' [39] But I say to you, Do not resist the one who is evil. But if anyone slaps you on the right cheek, turn to him the other also. [40] And if anyone would sue you and take your tunic, let him have your cloak as well. [41] And if anyone forces you to go one mile, go with him two miles. [42] Give to the one who begs from you, and do not refuse the one who would borrow from you.

[43] "You have heard that it was said, 'You shall love your neighbor and hate your enemy.' [44] But I say to you, Love your enemies and pray for those who persecute you, [45] so that you may be sons of your Father who is in heaven. For he makes his sun rise on the evil and on the good, and sends rain on the just and on the unjust. [46] For if you love those who love you, what reward do you have? Do not even the tax collectors do the same? [47] And if you greet only your brothers, what more are

you doing than others? Do not even the Gentiles do the same? 48 You therefore must be perfect, as your heavenly Father is perfect.

6 “Beware of practicing your righteousness before other people in order to be seen by them, for then you will have no reward from your Father who is in heaven.

2 “Thus, when you give to the needy, sound no trumpet before you, as the hypocrites do in the synagogues and in the streets, that they may be praised by others. Truly, I say to you, they have received their reward. 3 But when you give to the needy, do not let your left hand know what your right hand is doing, 4 so that your giving may be in secret. And your Father who sees in secret will reward you.

5 “And when you pray, you must not be like the hypocrites. For they love to stand and pray in the synagogues and at the street corners, that they may be seen by others. Truly, I say to you, they have received their reward. 6 But when you pray, go into your room and shut the door and pray to your Father who is in secret. And your Father who sees in secret will reward you.

7 “And when you pray, do not heap up empty phrases as the Gentiles do, for they think that they will be heard for their many words. 8 Do not be like them, for your Father knows what you need before you ask him. 9 Pray then like this:

“Our Father in heaven,
hallowed be your name.
10 Your kingdom come,
your will be done,
on earth as it is in heaven.
11 Give us this day our daily bread,
12 and forgive us our debts,
as we also have forgiven our debtors.
13 And lead us not into temptation,
but deliver us from evil.

14 For if you forgive others their trespasses, your heavenly Father will also forgive you, 15 but if you do not forgive others their trespasses, neither will your Father forgive your trespasses.

16 “And when you fast, do not look gloomy like the hypocrites, for they disfigure their faces that their fasting may be seen by others. Truly, I say to you, they have received their reward. 17 But when you fast, anoint your head and wash your face, 18 that your fasting may not be seen by others but by your Father who is in secret. And your Father who sees in secret will reward you.

19 “Do not lay up for yourselves treasures on earth, where moth and rust destroy and where thieves break in and steal, 20 but lay up for yourselves treasures in heaven, where neither moth nor rust destroys and where thieves do not break in and steal. 21 For where your treasure is, there your heart will be also.

22 “The eye is the lamp of the body. So, if your eye is healthy, your whole body will be full of light, 23 but if your eye is bad, your whole body will be full of darkness. If then the light in you is darkness, how great is the darkness!

24 “No one can serve two masters, for either he will hate the one and love the other, or he will be devoted to the one and despise the other. You cannot serve God and money.

25 “Therefore I tell you, do not be anxious
about your life, what you will eat or what you
will drink, nor about your body, what you will
put on. Is not life more than food, and the body
more than clothing? 26 Look at the birds of the
air: they neither sow nor reap nor gather into
barns, and yet your heavenly Father feeds them.
Are you not of more value than they? 27 And
which of you by being anxious can add a single
hour to his span of life? 28 And why are you
anxious about clothing? Consider the lilies of
the field, how they grow: they neither toil nor
spin, 29 yet I tell you, even Solomon in all his
glory was not arrayed like one of these. 30 But if
God so clothes the grass of the field, which
today is alive and tomorrow is thrown into the
oven, will he not much more clothe you, O you
of little faith? 31 Therefore do not be anxious,
saying, ‘What shall we eat?’ or ‘What shall we
drink?’ or ‘What shall we wear?’ 32 For the Gentiles seek after all these things, and your heavenly
Father knows that you need them all. 33 But seek
first the kingdom of God and his righteousness,
and all these things will be added to you.

34 “Therefore do not be anxious about tomorrow, for tomorrow will be anxious for
itself. Sufficient for the day is its own trouble.

7 “Judge not, that you be not judged. 2 For
with the judgment you pronounce you
will be judged, and with the measure you use
it will be measured to you. 3 Why do you see
the speck that is in your brother’s eye, but do
not notice the log that is in your own eye? 4 Or
how can you say to your brother, ‘Let me take
the speck out of your eye,’ when there is the
log in your own eye? 5 You hypocrite, first take
the log out of your own eye, and then you will
see clearly to take the speck out of your
brother’s eye.

6 “Do not give dogs what is holy, and do not
throw your pearls before pigs, lest they trample
them underfoot and turn to attack you.

7 “Ask, and it will be given to you; seek, and
you will find; knock, and it will be opened to
you. 8 For everyone who asks receives, and the
one who seeks finds, and to the one who
knocks it will be opened. 9 Or which one of
you, if his son asks him for bread, will give him
a stone? 10 Or if he asks for a fish, will give him
a serpent? 11 If you then, who are evil, know
how to give good gifts to your children, how
much more will your Father who is in heaven
give good things to those who ask him!

12 “So whatever you wish that others would
do to you, do also to them, for this is the Law
and the Prophets.

13 “Enter by the narrow gate. For the gate is
wide and the way is easy that leads to de-
struction, and those who enter by it are many.
14 For the gate is narrow and the way is hard
that leads to life, and those who find it are few.

15 “Beware of false prophets, who come
to you in sheep’s clothing but inwardly are
ravenous wolves. 16 You will recognize them
by their fruits. Are grapes gathered from
thornbushes, or figs from thistles? 17 So,
every healthy tree bears good fruit, but the
diseased tree bears bad fruit. 18 A healthy
tree cannot bear bad fruit, nor can a diseased tree bear good fruit. 19 Every tree that
does not bear good fruit is cut down and

thrown into the fire. 20 Thus you will recognize them by their fruits.

21 "Not everyone who says to me, 'Lord, Lord,' will enter the kingdom of heaven, but the one who does the will of my Father who is in heaven. 22 On that day many will say to me, 'Lord, Lord, did we not prophesy in your name, and cast out demons in your name, and do many mighty works in your name?' 23 And then will I declare to them, 'I never knew you; depart from me, you workers of lawlessness.'

24 "Everyone then who hears these words of mine and does them will be like a wise man who built his house on the rock. 25 And the rain fell, and the floods came, and the winds blew and beat on that house, but it did not fall, because it had been founded on the rock. 26 And everyone who hears these words of mine and does not do them will be like a foolish man who built his house on the sand. 27 And the rain fell, and the floods came, and the winds blew and beat against that house, and it fell, and great was the fall of it."

28 And when Jesus finished these sayings, the crowds were astonished at his teaching, 29 for he was teaching them as one who had authority, and not as their scribes.

INTRODUCTION

AN INVITATION TO FRUITFULNESS

After years of apartment living, an overseas move, first jobs, two small children, and nearly ten years of marriage, we bought our first house. It was perfect: huge picture windows, original wood floors, a yard for our children to play in, and a front porch where we envisioned sitting outside and chatting with neighbors as they walked by. The only challenge was that it had been a foreclosure and it needed a *ton* of work, especially on the outside. The yard, full of weeds and metal, wasn't quite what we envisioned our toddlers pushing trucks in or where we saw them running through the sprinklers.

In our yard, we dug out broken glass, found too-many-to-count beer-bottle caps, and uprooted years of overgrown bushes. We even let a neighborhood guy take his metal detector around to look for treasures (sadly, none were found!). Bryce recruited friends to help build a fence creating a safe space for kids to play. It took hours of labor, research, and plenty of muscle to begin making this house a home.

We loved sitting on our porch sipping a cold drink and talking with neighbors who expressed gratitude that we'd begun fixing up the house. But change took a whole lot longer than we thought, and it required intention, planning, and work. For the house and yard to become habitable, we needed the help, encouragement, and brawn of our friends to work alongside us too.

The same is true of our spiritual lives. Growth in the Christian life requires being acted on—like the ground being leveled and planted—so that something more life-giving can grow. Growth also requires others who work alongside you, and growth requires you follow a vision for what could be.

The Sermon on the Mount is Jesus' vision of the good life for his disciples (then and now). Such a life is fruitful: oriented to the flourishing of individuals and communities and a visible, tactile example that the kingdom of heaven has come in Jesus. Our lives as Jesus' followers are good new. They are like juicy pieces of fruit that testify to the goodness of life in Christ!

FRUITFULNESS IS GROWING TO LOOK MORE LIKE JESUS—LIVING AND LOVING AS HE DID.

When we talk about *fruitfulness* in this study, we mean "growing to look more like Jesus, living and loving as he did" (a phrase that both Dallas Willard and Steven Garber are fond of using). Toward the end of his most familiar sermon, known as the Sermon on the Mount, Jesus uses this same metaphor of fruitfulness and says that its by our fruits that people will be able to recognize us as Jesus' disciples (Matthew 7:20).

Healthy fruit comes from healthy plants (Matthew 7:17). But how does this happen? In John 15, Jesus uses this same fruit-bearing imagery: he calls himself the vine and says that his disciples (us!) are the branches. The Father is the gardener who prunes and cares for us so that we will bear fruit as we are attached to the vine, as we remain in Jesus. We are dependent on him, and we must remain connected to Jesus to grow. How do we remain *in* Jesus, like branches on a vine? Jesus says we do so by keeping his commands, some of which he lays out for us in the Sermon on the Mount (John 15:10). How can we do that? Through the work of the Spirit!

As we study Jesus' most famous sermon, and as we put it into practice, we expect that God's Spirit will work in our lives to grow spiritual fruit. That's Jesus' promise! Fruit bearing is evidence of being Jesus' disciple.

But this doesn't happen in an instant. Just as fruit trees take time before they produce fruit, growing to look more like Jesus takes time. Just like the transformation of our home, the cultivation of healthy spiritual fruit requires time with a vision, renewed intention, and a plan to get there. Ultimately our fruitfulness isn't just for us—it spills over so that our communities flourish too.

Fruitfulness also happens in stages. There will be seasons of fruit bearing, seasons when all you feel is God's pruning, and times of underground germination when all you can do is hope that roots are growing beneath the surface. All of this is normal. Through it all, we practice remaining connected to Jesus and his people.

Maybe you haven't cracked open a Bible in a while, or perhaps you're muscling through your Christian life but not experiencing growth. Either way, this study is for you. Dallas Willard often said that grace isn't opposed to effort, but it is opposed to earning. You'll be encouraged that Jesus fulfills all of what he's asking of you in himself, and you'll be challenged to make changes in your day-to-day life. Everything worth doing requires intention and effort. And in the Christian life, you know that the effort you put in flourishes because of the Holy Spirit who comforts, convicts, and promises to be the presence of Jesus with you.

As you begin this journey, take a moment to ask yourself what your hope is for this study. The process we're going to lead you through in this study is not magic. It won't just change you if you don't want to be transformed. Your intention is crucial. We can have initial enthusiasm when we begin something new, but then we falter. As you begin, consider, What are some areas you think you might struggle in? How can your group help support you?

A word about grace here—we will all fail. Our efforts are not about perfectionism or legalism. Jesus promises that his Word will not return void. He promises fruitful growth for healthy disciples. Imagine becoming calmer, gentler, less reactive, and more able to listen to God and others. We're going to be okay with being beginners, even if we know (or don't know!) a lot of Christian content. Let's expect that the Holy Spirit will cultivate us, working through the Word of God.

Each week as we meet together, we'll focus on the vision of the Sermon on the Mount and how Jesus tells us our highest aim and most secure self comes as we align ourselves with the kingdom of God. Here is real life, real fruit!

HOW TO USE THIS BOOK

Whether you are engaging in this study with a large group, a small group, in a coffee shop with a friend, or by yourself, here are some helpful suggestions.

FOR THE GROUP SESSION

Set aside a designated day and time for a weekly gathering—in person or virtually—for the next eight weeks. The content (video teaching, discussion, and prayer) will take about an hour to ninety minutes, depending on how much time you would like for discussion.

Videos are accessed through the QR code in the book. These videos were created with a group in mind. Ideally, you will watch the video together and then immediately engage in the content that follows. But because the videos are accessible through the QR code, each group member also has access, which is helpful if someone has to miss a group gathering.

Each group session will include these sections:

- **Begin**—We begin each session with two minutes of silence. This allows us to practice being with Jesus and each other, and calms our minds to encounter Scripture. Please read the appendix ("A Note on Silence") together at your first meeting. One member should open in prayer, and there's a beginning question to get conversation started (*5 minutes*).
- **Read**—Have a member of your group read the Scripture portion for that week out loud (*3-5 minutes*).
- **Watch**—Watch the video teaching together (*10-15 minutes*).
- **Discuss**—Use the discussion questions for the bulk of your time together (*25 minutes or more*).
- **Close**—We remind you weekly of God's grace to you in Jesus and ask for someone to close the group in prayer. Feel free to spend more time sharing requests and praying together here (*5-10 minutes*).

A few tips for group discussion:

- Be willing to participate in the discussion. The leader of your group will moderate the conversation, and it helps them to have willing participants.

- Be sensitive to other members and careful not to dominate the discussion. We are sometimes so eager to express our thoughts that we leave too little opportunity for others to respond. Be sure to make space for the insights of others.
- When possible, link what you say to the comments of others and the text. Be affirming whenever you can. Stick to the topic being discussed and try to avoid "rabbit trails."
- Expect God to teach you through the content being discussed and through the other members of the group.
- Pray that you will have an enjoyable and profitable time together, but also that as a result of the study, you will find ways that you can take action individually or even together as a group.
- Remember that anything said in the group is considered confidential and should not be discussed outside the group unless specific permission is given to do so.

We have designed these studies so that you could still participate in the group session even if you haven't done the individual days' work, but—of course—we think you'll still *want* to engage with all the content on individual days.

FOR THE INDIVIDUAL DAYS

Following the group session are five days of content for you to engage with on your own. We wrote this study with you in mind—the content is meaningful but not overwhelming, and it's designed to fit into your everyday life.

Each day, we ask you to read the passage of Scripture, spend a few minutes in silence, and think more deeply about the passage. Teaching sections are short and we encourage you to spend time applying the passage.

Each daily devotional time also includes a practice—a time to imaginatively engage Scripture and pray for God to grow the fruit of a disciple in your life. While some of these practices may be new for you, we encourage you to try them and find out what you discover about yourself, God, and others. We frequently invite you to write your responses, so you might want to use a journal alongside this workbook.

The rhythm of the individual days. Days 1-4 dig in to the content of the week's Scripture, and Day 5 focuses on Jesus' own fulfillment of the passage to remind you that we never earn or achieve a fruitful Christian life in our own effort.

You'll notice that the group session *starts* the week, so your participation doesn't hinge on completing your homework. Dive in, read the text, and may it fuel your time together and as you work through the content on subsequent days. Show up with your group even if you've missed a day (or all of them!). We hope and pray that your time will be fruitful!

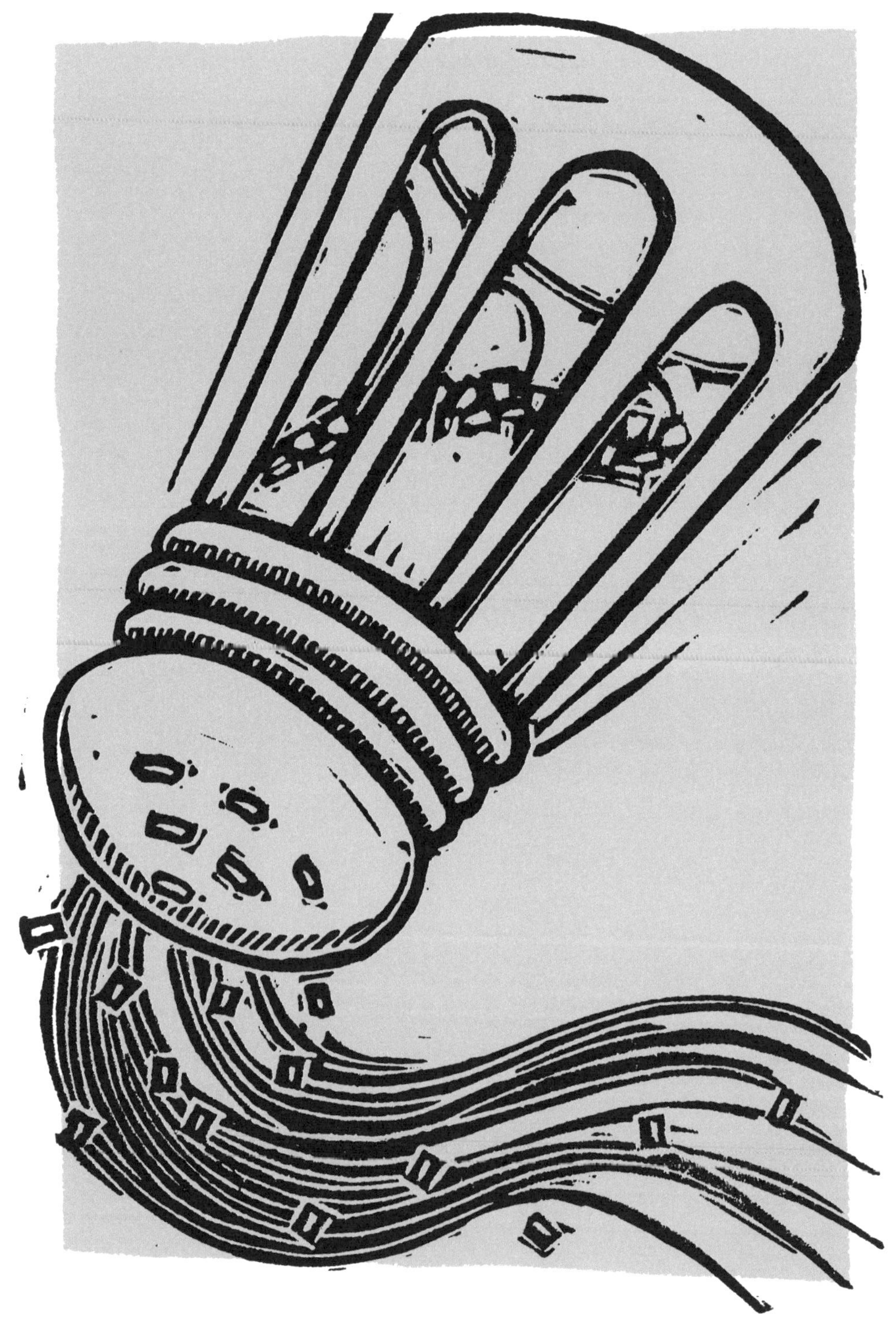

WEEK 1

THE FRUITFUL LIFE OF THE KINGDOM

MATTHEW 5:1-16

GROUP SESSION

BEGIN

- **Start** with two minutes of silence.
- **Pray** and invite the Spirit to be present, shaping you as people as you discuss.
- **Opening Question:** What has been forming you in the past week? (Take a look at your weekly phone usage for starters).

Throughout these weeks as we study the Sermon on the Mount, we will be practicing both individual and corporate times of silence. As this practice is new for many believers, we want to do our best to welcome you into this practice. Practicing silence is not akin to emptying your mind as in Eastern practices of meditation. It isn't prayer time either. It is a practice of slowing your body, mind, and soul to experience the reality and presence of God in a real time and a real place. In the same way that you need time together with a friend, we need unhurried time with God. (Please read the appendix at the end of the study for more information.)

READ

- **Read Matthew 5:1-16**

WATCH

- **Watch** video

DISCUSS

1. What has been your experience or first impression with the Sermon on the Mount? What was new for you in the video?
2. From your own experience, what makes a plant fruitful? What conditions are needed for fruit bearing? What things need to be taken away or added for healthy growth? See if you can make some connections between what you notice and your own life.
3. If you have a goal or dream for your life, or even the next few years, share it with the group. What goals do you have for your own spiritual growth? We want our lives to be effective (like

salt or light is effective), but often our dreams for living a good life don't look like Jesus' Beatitudes. Why do you think that is?

4. Look over Matthew 5:1-6. As you do, name the characteristics of someone Jesus says is blessed. Who, in your community or church, meets one or some of these characteristics?

5. From reading Matthew 5:13-16 and your own experience, what purpose does salt serve? Why might Jesus use this image of salt to talk about a fruitful disciple?

6. Considering verses 13-16 on salt and light, what characterizes a disciple of Jesus? What do they do and how do they act?

7. Take a look at this passage and notice the characteristics of people who Jesus values. Think about how you value time, attention, and money. What gaps do you notice between what you value and Jesus values?

8. Pick one area of your life in which you'd like to grow (a relationship, a need in your neighborhood, a new personal habit to try on, a new way of thinking, etc.). What's one small step you can take this week to grow in that area? How can your group support you?

CLOSE

Each week we'll remind you that the Sermon on the Mount isn't about doing more or getting it all correct. We will see some stark discrepancies between our desires and dreams and Jesus' model for fruitful discipleship. Finish your study each week in prayer, remembering that Jesus wants us to grow in our fruitfulness and that the way we become more fruitful disciples is by seeing his example, confessing our shortcomings, and loving him more fully for living on our behalf.

Jesus takes the pressure off. We do not need to get it right to be loved. Remind yourselves this week, while we re-evaluate, stretch, and grow, that—like tilling the soil—growing into a fruitful disciple can be hard. It also helps detach our identities from *what* we do to *whose* we are.

We'll also ask each week that you spend some time *praying together*. We've provided a written prayer below as a suggestion to help guide this time together.

Father, Son, and Holy Spirit, as we come to study Jesus' famous sermon we find ourselves excited and apprehensive. A fruitful life with you is our desire, and yet we know how great the gap is between the blessed life mentioned here and our own. As we study, reflect, and pray, would you remind us that the pressure is off—Jesus has accomplished our full redemption already and that the kingdom life he talks about in his sermon is actually the best life we could live? (Spend time here as appropriate praying for your week's next step.) *As we move forward into our weeks, grant us grace and the faith to believe what you say is true and good. We pray in the name of Christ Jesus our Lord, Amen.*

DAY 1 BEATITUDES, PART ONE

READ AND REFLECT

Each day we begin with two minutes of silence. Set a timer. Simply practice being in God's presence. The appendix in the back includes helpful suggestions.

→ **Read Matthew 5:1-6.** Read the passage slowly to yourself. Then, a second time if you're able, read it out loud.

We can think of Jesus' Sermon on the Mount as some nice words, a sort of spiritual fortune cookie. But Jesus actually preached the Sermon on the Mount in a real place, at a real time, among real people—people with questions and hungry bellies, people experiencing familial, economic, or political strife. As we enter into the text, try to remember the embodied reality of this sermon delivered out loud and out in the open to his first disciples on a hillside. Put yourself there.

Jesus' most famous sermon doesn't start with what people *should* do but instead starts with good news. He blesses before he commands. Grace comes before obedience. Jesus is quick to confer mercy on those who lack, who need help and sustenance, and on those who desire justice and righteousness like food and water.

- What words stand out to you when you read the passage? What is the effect of Jesus' repetitive language?

To be "poor in spirit" is to see our need for Jesus. Martyn Lloyd-Jones writes in *Studies in the Sermon on the Mount* that "poor in spirit" is having a "tremendous awareness of our utter nothingness as we come face to face with God."

- Think of a time when you have seen your utter need for God. What did that look and feel like?

- When have you seen an example of meekness displayed by someone else?

- We often think of a blessed life through the lens of accomplishments, status, or material security. What do these first three examples of who is a disciple (verses 3-5) tell us about what matters to God?

- As you read the text, what, if anything, is required to be a part of this fruitful life Jesus describes?

- In his commentary on Matthew, Frederick Dale Bruner reminds us that in this first section "Jesus sides with those who fail and who feel this failure." What is your reaction to this statement?

- It's hard to reckon with failure and lack. For what area of your life might the Holy Spirit be allowing you to see your failure as a place not only where Jesus meets you but also how this place is blessed? Write down some initial thoughts.

- In the Beatitudes, there is a promise at the end of each line that follows a need. How does this encourage you?

While we might approach these Beatitudes and see where we fall short, they're also, as Jonathan Pennington notes, funny—the incongruity between what sort of life we're striving for and what Jesus highlights. No one would expect that a meaningful, blessed life comes through lack. As there is humor in the space between expectation and reality, there is also grace in that spot too.

All fruitful faith is a gift.

JESUS' SERMON STARTS WITH GOOD NEWS.

PRACTICE

Each daily devotional time includes a practice section, a time to imaginatively engage Scripture and pray for God to grow the fruits of a disciple in your life.

As you read these opening verses again (Matthew 5:1-6), remember these are corporate blessings, given to "you all" and not just individuals. Who around you is mourning? Who is meek? Who is someone in your church or community who hungers after justice and righteousness? Imagine these people around you.

- **IMAGINE** Jesus seated on a hill, teaching his first followers. If you were there, how would you be showing up ready to listen to this teacher? As you imagine yourself and your community listening to Jesus, what do you hope Jesus will say?

- *Poor in spirit. Mourners. The meek. Those desperate for justice and righteousness.* What do these people have in common?

- How does Jesus meet these needs? How has he met these needs for you and your community?

- **PRAY** for a few minutes, bringing your whole self to God. Write down one intention or one impression from today's study to take with you.

DAY 2 BEATITUDES, PART TWO

READ AND REFLECT

- **Start** with two minutes of silence.
- **Read Matthew 5:7-12.** Read the passage slowly to yourself. Then, a second time if you're able, read it out loud.

- As you read these blessings, what questions about God and his kingdom do they bring up?

Often called the "help" Beatitudes, verses 7-9 show us that being in God's kingdom isn't just a vertical relationship between us and God, but it's also a horizontal relationship between us and people—as we show mercy, make peace, and practice discernment.

- Who around you, in your family, neighborhood, or community, needs mercy?

- In the Bible the word *shalom*, which we translate as "peace," means the wholeness of God. As you consider your neighborhood and church, where do they need God's wholeness and flourishing?

- Who are the helpers you know? How does helping others show you more of who God is?

- **Make a list** of the second half of each Beatitude (what comes after "for they shall . . ."). If we gather these promises together, what does it tell you about the experience of those who follow Jesus?

While we think the blessed life may look like ease and endless opportunities, Jesus tells us about hardship. If you feel your lack (as we see in the first few Beatitudes) and yet if you also move toward others (what we see here), persecution is the result (Matthew 5: 10-12). The type of kingdom Jesus brings is entirely different from the kingdoms of this world. Persecution and defeat mark not only Jesus' disciples but also Jesus himself—but still, there is always a promise of God's nearness and justice. The arc of redemption moves toward glory and victory, but this always comes on the other side of a cross.

- It doesn't seem to make sense, but how do you reconcile persecution as the pathway to a blessed life?

- Why do you think Jesus laid it out this way?

- Who is someone in your own life you can point to as lacking in conventional circumstances and yet blessed and full with Christ?

- What hope do you take from the Beatitudes for your life today?

PRACTICE

The phrase "pure in heart" is often taken to mean a clear-eyed seeing of God, oneself, and others. It's an unusual phrase, used only this one time. But it's a helpful phrase for our approach to reading Scripture. We want to see God more clearly—to not only know more about him but *know* him more.

Sometimes we can get overly familiar with biblical words or stories. Try reading the Beatitudes in a different translation than you usually use by grabbing another Bible if you have it or using an online search, such as BibleGateway.

- What change in wording in this version grabbed your attention? How did the alternate reading affect your understanding of the passage? Bring these to God in prayer and ask for the Spirit to illuminate the parts that are hard to hear or understand. Write down a few thoughts.

DAY 3 THE SALT OF THE EARTH

READ AND REFLECT

- **Start** with two minutes of silence.
- **Read Matthew 5:13.**

The Beatitudes give us Jesus' blessing for the least of these and for those who help others. They show us the width of who Jesus calls blessed in his kingdom. This section shows us how Jesus' disciples are also particular. They are to be God's presence in the world as salt and light.

As we discussed in the group session, salt is a seasoning, a preservative, and was even precious enough to be used as currency. As a preservative, it keeps what is good and whole intact, so meat doesn't spoil. It's a seasoning too; it makes food taste better. In the ancient world, salt was even used as a currency. It was valuable; it's why we talk about someone being "worth their salt." Ancient trading routes, called "salt ways," popped up before proper roads did, to bring salt from oceans and rivers inland across hundreds of miles.

- What is the significance of Jesus calling his followers "the salt of the earth"?

- Jesus didn't say that his followers had to figure out how to be salt or to work hard in order to be salt. He said they *are* salt. What's the difference between *being* salt or working hard *to be* salt?

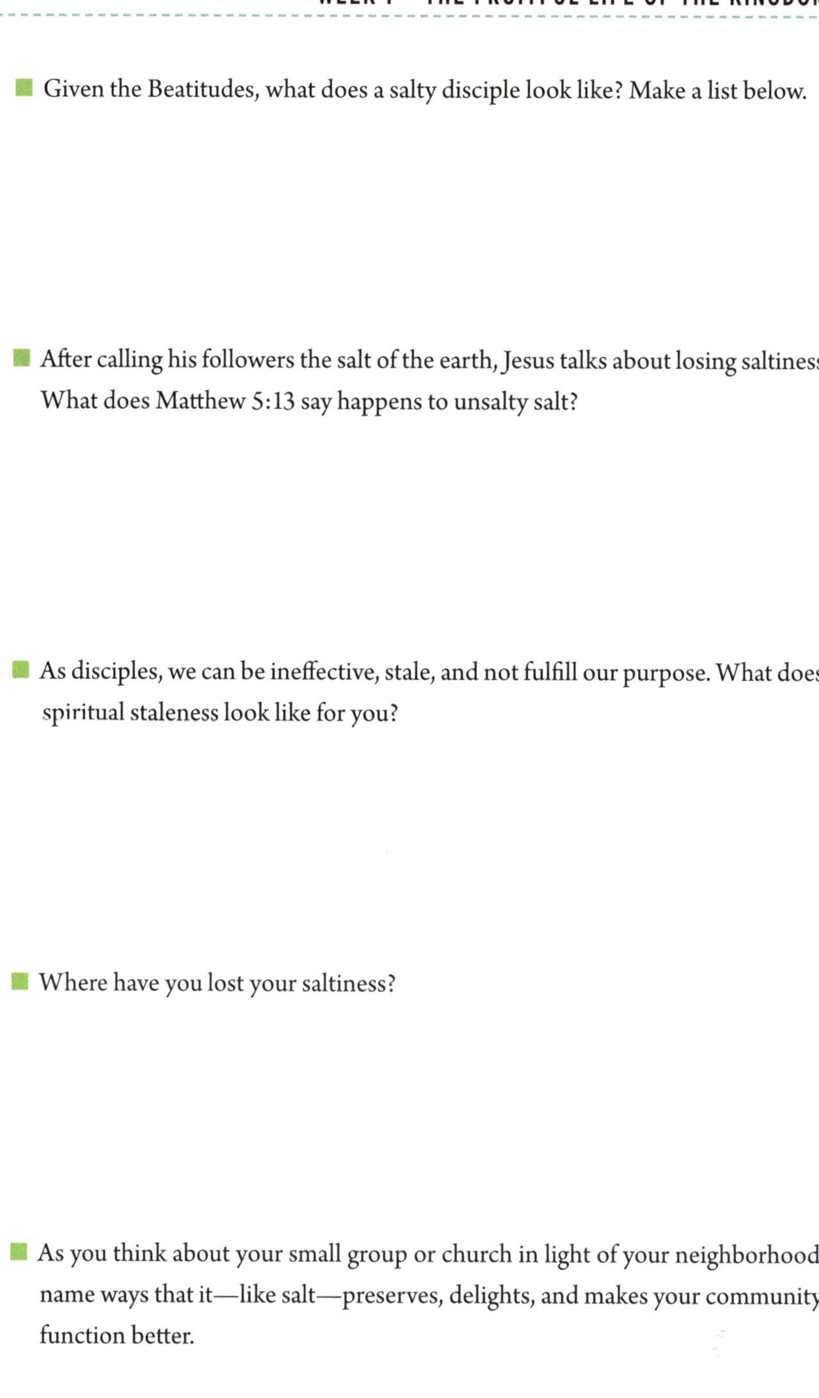

- Given the Beatitudes, what does a salty disciple look like? Make a list below.

- After calling his followers the salt of the earth, Jesus talks about losing saltiness. What does Matthew 5:13 say happens to unsalty salt?

- As disciples, we can be ineffective, stale, and not fulfill our purpose. What does spiritual staleness look like for you?

- Where have you lost your saltiness?

- As you think about your small group or church in light of your neighborhood, name ways that it—like salt—preserves, delights, and makes your community function better.

PRACTICE

The following practice is meant to be a way to gently engage these hard questions as you seek to receive God's grace—which is made clear in the phrases beginning with "you are"—and recognize where you fall short, as well. Before you begin, ask the Holy Spirit to be with you.

Many modern roads began as ancient salt ways. These salt ways were created to bring salt from a body of water inland, both for the health of a people and for economic stability.

If Christians are the salt of the earth, we're going to consider moments when our flavor has been strong—when we've seasoned our places and people and preserved goodness—and when we have lost our flavor.

- Using the map below, in company with the Holy Spirit, write down a few events, memories, or feelings where faith in Jesus was vital, strong, and precious (like valuable salt in the ancient world), and mark these along the waterway at the green markers.
- On the orange markers, write down times, events, or seasons when your saltiness has decreased. Consider, from your current vantage point, whether the less salty times were times of fallowness and growth later resulted, or times you distanced yourself from God.
- **CONSIDER** how these seasons of growth and fallowness are like the growth cycles for a plant. Both are necessary. What patterns do you notice?

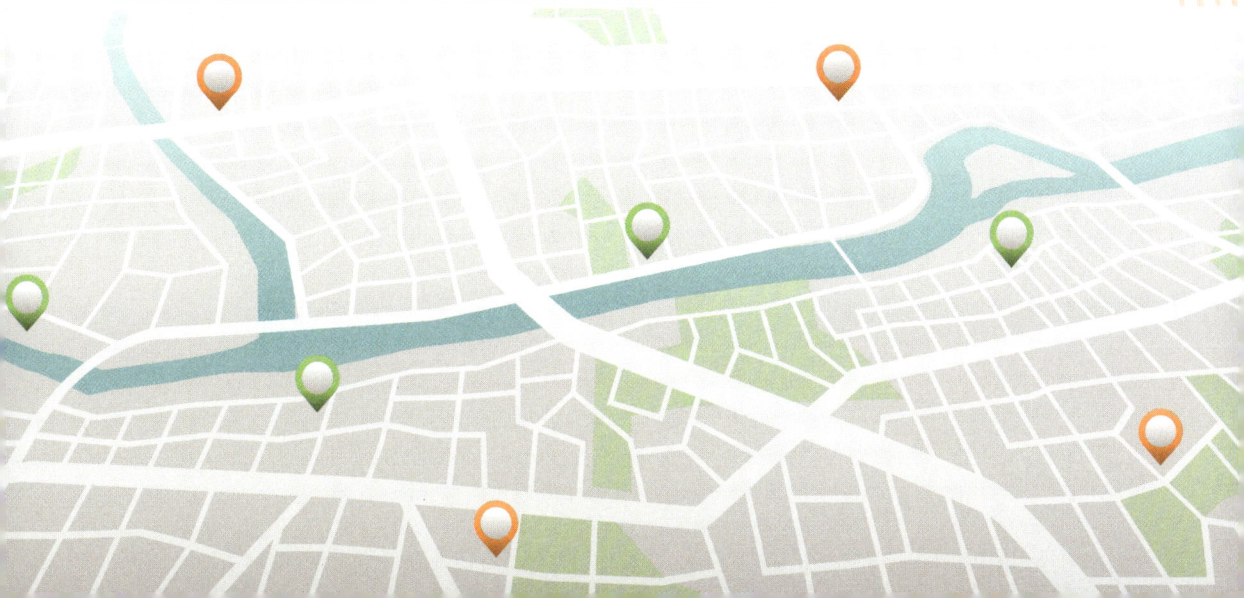

Finally, spend some time in prayer, and practice being honest with God—the good, the hard, the pain, the places where you have numbed or run away from him. He knows it already. Pray through each orange and green marker, the memories of connection to God at the waterway, and ask him to grow your faith.

DAY 4 THE LIGHT OF THE WORLD

READ AND REFLECT

- **Start** with two minutes of silence.
- **Read Matthew 5:14-16.**

Before the advent of electricity, travelers to Jerusalem would've been restricted to natural sources of light and the moon's cycles. When they got there, God orchestrated that the Jewish festivals would take place during a full moon for maximum enjoyment with maximum light, allowing God's people to celebrate long into the evenings together.

Throughout Scripture, light is used to reference physical light but is also used more poetically to signal holiness, perfection, purity, and goodness.

- **Read 1 Timothy 6:16.** How is light connected with God in this verse?

Light creates the conditions for flourishing, for celebration, for shalom—the Bible's word not just for the absence of conflict but also for the fullness of what life ought to be. Pause for a few moments and think about the beauty, power, and utility of light.

> LIGHT CREATES THE CONDITIONS FOR FLOURISHING, FOR CELEBRATION, FOR SHALOM.

- What are a few words you use to describe light?

You are salt. You are light. Nothing can take away the fact that you are salt and you are light. You don't need to earn your status as salt or light. Your life is meant to preserve what is good, true, just, and beautiful, so these do not spoil. You are to illuminate the darkness and live in such a way that your light shines before men and they glorify your Father in heaven (see 1 Peter 2:12 for more).

- One way to think about a light-filled Christian is that we're drawn to them, like beautiful light. What does this look like in your home, at work, in your neighborhood?

- Can you think of some examples of light-filled people you know?

- What if there was a whole group of people committed to doing just that? How would it change the culture of your church or city?

But now the hard part: light, like salt, can be less than what it was created to be. It can be dimmed or hidden. We're peeling back the layers between what Jesus says makes a fruitful Christian life in God's kingdom and where we have been less than what we were created to be.

For fruit to grow in our lives—for us to really act like light-filled Christians—we must begin with an accurate assessment of where we are.

- Where have you found your faith dim?

- When you see this in yourself, do you move toward God (the source of light) or away? And if you answered, "away," how might the Beatitudes invite you back?

PRACTICE

We're so used to electric lighting that it feels foreign to go without light. For today's practice, here are a few suggestions to help you practice paying attention to light. Pick one and reflect:

- After sundown, eat a meal by candlelight without any electric lights. Try using only candlelight for the evening. Observe your experience with limited light.
- Take a walk and notice how the light changes or how it filters through clouds or trees.
- Light a candle as you pray. Pay attention to how the flame flickers. Place the candle in different corners of the room to see how the light splashes around the room.
- Find a beautiful painting and study the light. (*Girl with a Pearl Earring* by Vermeer or Rembrandt's *Self-Portrait* [1659] are some great examples.) Notice where the light comes from, what is hidden, and what is illuminated.

Whichever practice you choose, consider how you might imagine God's people as a light to the world. Spend some time in prayer telling God what you've learned about light and invite his light into your life.

DAY 5 JESUS DOES THE WORK FOR US

READ AND REFLECT

→ **Start** with two minutes of silence.

In our Day 5 readings and reflection we'll zoom out a bit to summarize and see how Jesus doesn't just deliver the Sermon on the Mount, but he also embodies it. Each week during the Day 5 lesson, we spend time meditating on the ways Jesus fulfills the Sermon on the Mount and shows us what a fruitful life looks like.

Throughout the Gospels, Jesus embodies the Beatitudes: He works for justice. He's angry at religious leaders who neglect prayer and the poor. He hungers and thirsts for righteousness in his study of the Hebrew Scriptures and in his regular prayer life. He has mercy on those he heals and is meek, "like a lamb that is led to the slaughter," as he embraces the cross (Isaiah 53:7).

→ **Read Matthew 4:16; John 1:4; John 1:9; and Revelation 22:5.**

- How does each passage link Jesus with light? Write down some thoughts.

  → Matthew 4:16:

  → John 1:4:

  → John 1:9:

  → Revelation 22:5:

- **Notice** the similarities and differences between the way each passage speaks about Jesus as the light. What is similar? What is different in each passage?

- What conclusions can you draw from these similarities and differences?

You are the salt of the earth. You are the light of the world—because Jesus is salt and light first and we are in him!

Jesus' own life shows us what light looks like: light shines in the darkness. It illuminates our fears, broken systems, and dark hearts. But Jesus is not afraid of our darkness. He comes to show us the way, the way back into living in the light. When we are in darkness, the light of God is what we need to find true and abundant life. Let us step into the light of Christ.

- **Write down** a few ways God has provided insight about this portion of Scripture and your own life this week. What has he illuminated?

Paul writes in his letter to the Ephesians: "At one time you were darkness, but now you are light in the Lord. Walk as children of light" (Ephesians 5:8).

- How did Paul's hearers become children of light?

- What do you think it means to walk as children of light?

PRACTICE

Take heart: Jesus is the light of the world. You are united with him, and through the power of the Spirit, you are invited into the light that is for the whole world.

- **PRAY** and ask the Spirit to be a light in your darkness so that you would experience the light of Christ for you and in you. Here are some prompts to help you pray:

  → *Father, your Word tells us that we are blessed when we are in need. Here are the places where I lack:*

  → *Jesus, what you promise in the Sermon on the Mount is a radical reframing of what I think of as a successful or good life. As I consider what a fruitful and resilient disciple is while reading this portion of Scripture, I think:*

  → *Holy Spirit, would you show me in my life today where my lack can be filled up with Christ's fullness? I bring before you the parts of my day now:*

WEEK 2

FRUITFULNESS AND GOD'S LAW

MATTHEW 5:17-37

GROUP SESSION

BEGIN

- START with two minutes of silence.
- PRAY and invite the Spirit to be present, shaping you as people as you discuss.
- OPENING QUESTION: What has been a motivator to help you change a habit in the past?

READ

- READ MATTHEW 5:17-37

WATCH

- WATCH video

DISCUSS

1. Think of a resolution you made (either recently or a while ago). What caused it to stick or fail?
2. Many people see Jesus' commands as too strict or too impossible to keep. How realistic are Jesus' instructions? Why would he have given them if they're so hard to enact?
3. Is there something new in the video teaching that helps clarify how to read the Sermon on the Mount?
4. What, do you think, it means to "abolish the Law or the Prophets"? Does this mean we can live however we want? Where in your cultural context or in yourself do you see this desire to either ignore the law or strenuously try to meet its requirements? Share one specific example.
5. If Jesus is not abolishing the law, then what might he be doing when he uses the phrase, "You have heard that it was said . . . But I say . . ."?
6. Let's look at one section and apply it. What is something that prompted an angry response from you this week? Are there other emotions underneath the anger?

7. In verses 27-30, Jesus notes that the betrayal of adultery is seen not only physically but also in a desire to live outside proper boundaries. Where might you notice unconstrained desire in your life? How have you tried to tame that?

8. Considering the new commandments on divorce and taking oaths in the Sermon on the Mount, what can we learn about how we should treat others?

9. Consider the ways in which Jesus lives out his words in the Sermon on the Mount as he goes to the cross. How do you see Jesus embodying this restrained approach to anger as he refuses to answer his accusers? How did he constrain his desires as he prays to the Father, "Not my will, but yours, be done"? How does he remain true to his word?

10. In our study of the Sermon on the Mount, we're seeing that Jesus' words are a road map for living a fruitful life as his disciples. Discuss with your group how Jesus' teaching on the "Law and the Prophets" contributes to a fruitful life. Remember, when we talk about fruitfulness we mean increasingly looking like Jesus and becoming characterized by the fruit of the Spirit.

11. What is the use of the law? Why might it be good for a person or for a society? How has this section affected your understanding of God's Word in your life?

CLOSE

Remember: Jesus takes the pressure off. His law is a gracious invitation to love him more fully.

Close by spending some time in prayer. Here are some suggestions to get you started:

Thank you, Father, for revealing yourself in your Word. Here's what I'm realizing about your good law . . .

God, when I read these moral commands, I realize how far away my actions are. I realize the gap between what I say I believe and my internal motivations . . .

Thank you, Jesus, that you fulfill the law on our behalf. Most of the time I live without thinking about your law or try to make excuses. Help me stand secure in Jesus' perfect record.

DAY 1 THE LAW FULFILLED

READ AND REFLECT

- **Start** with two minutes of silence.
- **Read Matthew 5:17-20.**

If the Beatitudes show us that we're blessed when we are weak and lowly, it's easy to think that the love Jesus offers means that the Old Testament law no longer applies. We think freedom is the absence of constraints. This impulse is understandable: if less is required, perhaps we can meet those expectations and merit the great love of God. Let's consider how Jesus' words might reshape our assumptions about living a fruitful life and discover its connection to God's law.

- **Read Matthew 5:17-20 again.** Try to list three or more things Jesus says about the Old Testament.

- What are some of the ways you tend to relax God's commandments? Why do you think you are prone to do so?

- **Read** verse 20. We don't tend to think of the Pharisees as commendable people. What does Jesus mean by saying that our righteousness must exceed theirs?

Here, as elsewhere, what precedes this part of the sermon informs how we meditate on these verses today. The same Jesus who told his followers just a moment ago that they were the light of the world and salt of the earth calls his disciples to actually live as salt and light, not just think or talk about it. We must live into our blessedness before we have the capacity to understand and honor God's law.

- How do you experience being one of God's blessed people?

- **Name** some examples of God's love changing and shaping you.

When we are loved and safe, we have courage to change. And our tendency to lessen the sting of the law or to even surround it with extra rules (as did the Pharisees) effectively distances us from intimacy with Jesus. Imagine what would happen if every time one of us asked, "Please pick up your clothes off the floor of our bedroom," the other ignored the request. We'd feel hurt and unloved. But love motivates us toward change and action.

When we water down the law of God or even try to keep it by making extra laws so we don't break the *real* one, we don't honor God's Word. The law is a guardrail given by God to invite you into an integrated, fruitful life in his kingdom.

> **THE LAW IS A GUARDRAIL GIVEN BY GOD TO INVITE YOU INTO AN INTEGRATED, FRUITFUL LIFE IN HIS KINGDOM.**

- Based on what Jesus says in these verses, how do you think the law of God shows us what a fruitful life looks like?

Jesus says he has come to fulfill the law. He also says that our righteousness must exceed that of the Pharisees. At first glance, these two statements may seem to contradict each other. In his life, Jesus perfectly obeys for you all that the law requires, and in his death, he pays the penalty for your disobeying God's law. He is therefore perfectly righteous, and he gives his righteousness to you through his sacrificial death on the cross.

- In light of the truth that Jesus fulfills the law on your behalf in his life and death, how do you understand his teaching that your righteousness must exceed "that of the scribes and Pharisees"? How does one enter the kingdom of heaven?

- How could the reality of Jesus' perfect righteousness given freely to you transform the way you seek to obey God's law?

PRACTICE

One way God's law works is by exposing how much we need a Savior. Close your eyes and imagine a tree planted by streams of fresh and flowing water. Get a good sense of what it looks like and how it would feel to be in its comforting shade. Activate your senses to imagine this place in your mind's eye. A tree's growth corresponds to its immense, healthy, and connected root structure.

As you consider this tree, read these words by Frederick Dale Bruner in his commentary on this passage: we need a Savior's forgiveness that reaches "beneath our will, underneath our sinful acts, and covers our sinful *nature*, our subterranean *drives*, our *original* sin, our depths."

Open your hands in a posture of receiving. Ask the Holy Spirit to illuminate your own root structure. Does the mercy and fullness of Jesus reach down to your heart's roots? Are you stuck on a treadmill of endlessly doing more to try to fulfill God's law or a law you've made up? Spend two minutes listening in silence to what God is saying to you.

Receive the fullness of Christ and his blessing on your behalf. If you'd like, journal about your experience.

DAY 2 ANGER

READ AND REFLECT

→ **Start** with two minutes of silence.

→ **Read Matthew 5:21-26.**

It's said that anger is a secondary emotion. We often erupt or stew in anger, but there's usually something deeper. Underneath our unrighteous anger may be fear, sadness, embarrassment, confusion, shame, disgrace, or a sense of being unseen.

- What seems to trigger your anger? Take a couple of minutes to list several things that make you angry.

- What do the things that make you angry reveal to you about the state of your own heart?

When we use our words or actions in unrighteous anger, we are defacing or murdering the image of God in ourselves (when our anger is pointed inward) and others (when our anger is pointed outward). We can excuse our anger by trying to wiggle our way out of God's law or calling down the justice of God on others, but Jesus says that the kingdom of God so upends our lives that we become less self-protective, less angry people. How is this possible?

→ **Read Matthew 5:23-26** again.

- What is the connection between anger and our worship of God? What actions does Jesus say should characterize his disciples with a fellow believer (v. 23) and an "accuser" (vv. 24-26)?

In Isaiah 53, eight hundred years before the birth of Christ, the prophet predicts that the Messiah would be misunderstood and unjustly punished. Indeed, we see Jesus—in a sham trial in the middle of the night before he is sentenced to crucifixion—refusing to defend himself from the unjust actions of his accusers. He suffers in silence. Isaiah says, "He was oppressed, and he was afflicted, yet he opened not his mouth; like a lamb that is led to the slaughter, and like a sheep that before its shearers is silent, so he opened not his mouth" (Isaiah 53:7).

- What does Jesus silently suffering injustice tell us about the way he handled his anger? What does this mean for you?

We'll see later in the sermon that Jesus says that healthy trees cannot help but produce healthy fruit. Our anger that is unrighteous, then, is the fruit of our heart's soil. When we are angry, we value our own rights, our own control, our own perspective over love of God and love of neighbor. Who hasn't called someone a jerk when they were cut off on a highway? Who hasn't thought of someone as stupid who disagreed with your assessment? Jesus' kingdom life isn't just a matter of right action—fewer angry outbursts—but more than that, he's creating fruitful, healthy hearts in us. And in so doing, he is also exposing our poor root structures, our faltering fruit, and our shallow soil. When we are angry, we tend to minimize our faults and emphasize the ways we have been wronged, but gratitude turns this tendency upside down.

- Take a few minutes to list as many things as you can for which you are grateful to God.

- How does reflecting on things for which you are grateful transform your anger and frustration?

The passage from Isaiah 53 we mentioned earlier in today's study reminds us that Jesus suffered injustice without complaint. The injustice he suffered includes paying for sins that we committed.

- Take a few moments to confess your anger to him, and then thank him for paying your debt, rather than reacting in anger.

PRACTICE

PRAY and spend an extended time in silence and solitude today, perhaps ten minutes or more—before bed, on a lunch break, or even in your bathroom. Ask the Spirit to show you your own anger: where it comes from, what it's trying to protect, what's underneath it. Write down below what you learn about yourself and God's kind provision.

DAY 3 LUST: UNCONSTRAINED DESIRE

READ AND REFLECT

- **Start** with two minutes of silence.
- **Read Matthew 5:27-30.**

When we are angry at another person, we use our power over them: it is the same with lust. Lust is a matter not just of sexual immorality but also of reducing another human being who bears the image of God to an object to be used for our own gratification.

- Why does Jesus speak about cutting off hands or gouging out eyes? What do you think his purpose is in speaking so forcefully?

In talking about lust, Jesus speaks here about what we do with both our eyes and our hands—what we see *and* what we do. Both can cause us to stumble.

- Jesus is not speaking only about sexual lust here. What are some ways that you objectify others in what you see and what you do?

- Most scholars agree that Jesus is not encouraging people to mutilate themselves. How, then, should we understand Jesus' statement that "it is better that you lose one of your members than that your whole body go into hell" (v. 30)?

- We live in a world where we are bombarded by images, often of a very sexual and provocative nature. Spend a moment thinking through the seriousness of God's holy law and your reaction to it. What might it look like for you to consider the gravity of your own sin? What would it look like to stop, repent, and run from lust?

Jesus' commands in this section of the Sermon on the Mount show us the perfection of God's intention for the human race. The commands also show us that none can stand before him. We are angry. We are lustful, and we do not even know how to diminish our drives and desires so that we can be pure as Jesus commands his disciples to be. If the Beatitudes lift up the lowly, the commands we are considering this week knock us down—pointing out our need for a Savior. Think of these commands as Jesus plowing the hard soil of our hearts.

IF THE BEATITUDES LIFT UP THE LOWLY, THE COMMANDS WE ARE CONSIDERING THIS WEEK KNOCK US DOWN—POINTING OUT OUR NEED FOR A SAVIOR.

- Can you think of times when Jesus honored the humanity of an individual instead of using them for his own purposes? List a few below:

As he hangs on the cross, the soldiers, rulers, and even one of the thieves hanging next to him taunt Jesus, saying, "If you are the King of the Jews, save yourself" (see Luke 23:32-43). Instead of gratifying himself and coming down from the cross, however, Jesus willingly surrenders his desires, comfort, even his life to serve us! Rather than lustfully using others to satisfy himself, he gives himself up to save us.

- How does Jesus' sacrifice change the way you think about your desires for pleasure, comfort, success, or something else?

- How might Jesus' sacrifice for you transform the way you respond the next time you are seized with lustful desire?

PRACTICE

In the beginning pages of Andy Crouch's book *The Life We're Looking For*, he speaks about a walking spiritual exercise he undertook in an airport. Especially in an airport, getting from point A to point B can mean we view those in our path as impediments.

Instead of this, he chose to walk around the airport and as he passed each person, he would look them in the eye and say in his mind, *image bearer*. Today as you pass cars, your family and friends, and your colleagues, choose to look them in the eye and say, "image bearer."

DAY 4 INTEGRITY: DIVORCE AND OATHS

READ AND REFLECT

- **START** with two minutes of silence.
- **READ MATTHEW 5:31-37.**

Over the last couple of days we've thought about Jesus' words concerning anger and lust, which get to the hidden desires that drive us. Today we're considering this section on divorce and oaths, which points us outward to the integrity we have interacting with others.

- By using the word "again" in verse 33, Jesus is saying that his teaching on divorce in verses 31-32 parallels his teaching on oaths in verses 33-37. How would you summarize Jesus' teaching in this section in a sentence or two?

- In the culture of Jesus' time, women were vulnerable and often dependent on a husband for safety, shelter, and sustenance. How does this reality deepen our understanding of Jesus' words in verse 37?

- We now live in a time where roughly 50 percent of marriages last throughout a couples' lifetime. What is your reaction to these commands?

Paul later writes about marriage in Ephesians 5, saying that the unity of husband and wife in marriage is a "profound mystery." Reading the passage below, what does marriage point to (see the last sentence, verse 32)?

Husbands, love your wives, as Christ loved the church and gave himself up for her, that he might sanctify her, having cleansed her by the washing of water with the word, so that he might present the church to himself in splendor, without spot or wrinkle or any such thing, that she might be holy and without blemish. In the same way husbands should love their wives as their own bodies. He who loves his wife loves himself. For no one ever hated his own flesh, but nourishes and cherishes it, just as Christ does the church, because we are members of his body. "Therefore a man shall leave his father and mother and hold fast to his wife, and the two shall become one flesh." This mystery is profound, and I am saying that it refers to Christ and the church. (Ephesians 5:25-32)

- What are some messages you receive about the purpose of marriage?

- What is God's purpose for marriage?

- How do Jesus' words about keeping our promises in marriage and Paul's teaching that marriage is a picture of God's faithfulness to us affect your understanding of what it means to be true to your word?

PRACTICE

Jesus not only teaches us about integrity in our interactions with others, but he also modeled it in the way he lived. **READ MATTHEW 9:18-26**, where he demonstrates care for a woman and a young girl. Take some time to reflect on the following questions:

- How does Jesus affirm the value and dignity of each person in this account?
- How does he uphold the standards of God's law?
- How do others in this narrative respond to Jesus?

- **WRITE:** Spend some time journaling your own reactions to Jesus' law and confess where you need his help.

DAY 5 JESUS FULFILLS THE LAW FOR US

READ AND REFLECT

- **Start** with two minutes of silence.

On Day 5 we spend some time meditating on the ways Jesus fulfills the Sermon on the Mount and shows us what a fruitful life looks like.

In all Jesus did, thought, acted on, and preached, and in all times—in his moments alone, in his moments with outcasts and sinners, in his moments with high-ranking officials—he had perfect integrity. His yes was yes. He respected and valued all people. He upheld his word. He called for perfect purity of body, heart, soul, and mind.

Before Jesus' Sermon on Mount, Matthew 4 recounts Jesus' temptations in the wilderness. Here Satan tempts Jesus to provide for his own physical needs, to use his power for his own gain, and to worship Satan in a bid for worldly prestige. These temptations, if given in to, would gratify the desires of the flesh, use people and angels for his own ends, and cause Jesus to lack integrity between the mission he spoke of and how he acted.

In the temptations, Jesus understands how we are tempted to gratify our fleshly desires, to make people into objects, to display our power, and to choose to be less than upright because it means getting ahead. In the temptations, Jesus models for us a life of resilient faithfulness to God and to his Word. The fruitfulness of his own obedience was on display: the roots held, the branch was buffeted, and the fruit was holy.

- How does considering Jesus' actions in Matthew 4 deepen our appreciation for his teaching in Matthew 5?

- How does Jesus respond to the temptations of the accuser in Matthew 4? What words does he quote?

- How does Jesus' use of God's Word inform the way we respond to temptation?

Take a minute to reflect on the perfect law of God. At the beginning of the Ten Commandments, God says, "I am the LORD your God, who brought you out of the land of Egypt, out of the house of slavery. You shall have no other gods before me" (Exodus 20:2-3). God doesn't just free us from destructive ways of acting but also from spiritual slavery! It is in the context of relationship and tender care that he gives his law.

- Think about all the ways you've tried to keep God's law, or even a New Year's resolution. When willpower gave out, what did you turn to? Does shame motivate you to change? What was helpful or unhelpful to you in keeping this?

- How might God's words here affect the way we approach obedience?

Pray and reflect on God's perfect law and perfect provision of Jesus as a Savior who gives you his perfect record. Praise him and ask for help to follow in the ways he says make a fruitful life.

- What can you praise him for? Where has he shown himself faithful in your life?
- Where does his Word confront you? What can you confess to him?
- How does he meet your need in Christ? How is Jesus the answer to your confession?
- Thank him for the way he meets you in Christ and guides you as you seek to follow him.

PRACTICE

REFLECT on this past week's study of God's law. We cannot ultimately cause spiritual fruit to grow in our hearts, but we can prepare the soil by paying attention to God's Word, repenting of the ways we fall short, looking to Christ in faith, and intentionally seeking to follow him.

> THE FRUITFUL LIFE WE DESIRE TAKES TIME. AS EUGENE PETERSON SAID, IT'S A LONG OBEDIENCE IN THE SAME DIRECTION.

It's worth remembering that the fruitful life we desire takes time. As Eugene Peterson said, it's a long obedience in the same direction.

THINK of one or two commands in Scripture (perhaps from this study) that you have struggled to keep in the past. What was helpful in this struggle to keep the law? What was unhelpful?

What would it feel like to no longer struggle with this particular command—if it were easy to keep? How, then, is keeping God's law good for you and for others?

PRAY about and reflect on God's law, practicing gratitude for Jesus' fulfillment of the law, and exploring how keeping God's law brings freedom.

WEEK 3

FRUITFULNESS IS JUSTICE AND MERCY

MATTHEW 5:38–6:4

GROUP SESSION

BEGIN

- **Start** with two minutes of silence.
- **Pray** and invite the Spirit to be present, shaping you as people as you discuss.
- **Opening Question:** When have you found yourself getting upset in the past week? What have you learned about yourself and God's law?

READ

- **Read Matthew 5:38–6:4**

WATCH

- **Watch** video

DISCUSS

1. Think of a recent time when you have appealed for your rights. Share one incident with the group.
2. What is your reaction regarding the standard of "an eye for an eye"? Is mere justice enough, or do we want more than justice from others?
3. Jesus commands his followers to give more than is required, to respond to insults with kindness, and to love those who hate. How do you react to this?
4. Are Jesus' words in this passage realistic? Why or why not?
5. What is the difference between justice and mercy?
6. It's important for us to remember that Jesus does more than tell us to love our enemies, go the extra mile, and repay insults with kindness. As we respond to Jesus' teaching us to treat others this way, we must remember that we have been treated this way by God. Discuss the ways in which God has shown you mercy rather than merely giving you what you deserve. Be specific.

7. How does remembering that we have first received mercy from God reorient our perspective and motivate us to show mercy to others?

8. Think about the week ahead of you. What are some situations you may find yourself in or people you will encounter that rub you the wrong way? How might this study affect the way you interact with these circumstances?

9. How is the perfection required in verse 48 part of the fruit of the radical nature of God's grace in the life of his disciples? How does this verse make sense within the context of the Sermon on the Mount as a whole?

10. What difference do you think it would make in your world if Jesus' people embodied the ethic of mercy instead of merely an ethic of justice?

11. What's one small step you can take in the coming week to make the ethic of mercy your default response?

CLOSE

Remember that Jesus takes the pressure off.

Pray together in smaller groups. You may use the following for prayer prompts if desired:

God, I praise and thank you for giving us mercy . . .

Father, this ethic of mercy is not something I can accomplish by willpower. I need you . . .

As I consider my upcoming week, I know that I'm often only concerned about my own rights. Help me . . .

Lord, my gratitude muscle is weak. Help me pay attention to small ways you show up and help me to practice being thankful.

DAY 1 THE IMPULSE TO RETALIATE

READ AND REFLECT

- START with two minutes of silence.
- READ MATTHEW 5:38-42.

- REREAD verse 39. What is Jesus asking of his followers? What is your reaction to Jesus' "but I say to you" command here?

We live in a time and place where it is generally assumed that all people should be treated justly, regardless of their background or social standing. Because of this expectation, we have a hard time with the word *retaliation*. Surely we would never gouge out someone's eye or knock out their tooth. The idea of getting even with someone who has hurt us sounds juvenile at best, perhaps even barbaric. But let's take a closer look.

- READ EXODUS 21:23-27. How did this "eye for an eye" ethic keep communities together? What protection can you see that it would offer those who were especially vulnerable?

- Is Matthew 5 saying something different from Exodus 21?

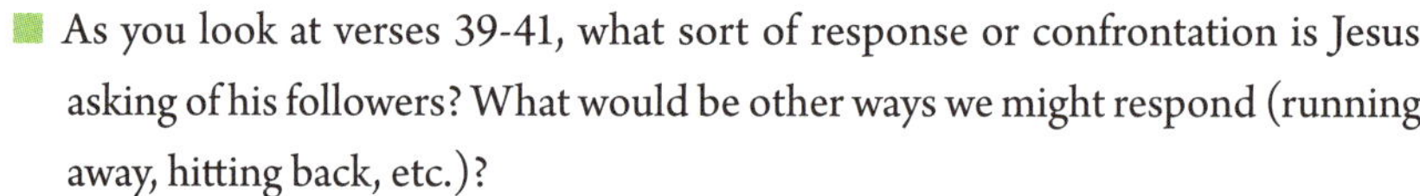

- As you look at verses 39-41, what sort of response or confrontation is Jesus asking of his followers? What would be other ways we might respond (running away, hitting back, etc.)?

If the Sermon on the Mount shows us how Jesus is more concerned about the transformed, fruitful, and resilient character of his followers, it's possible we could follow the letter of the law but actually be unchanged internally. We could be plants with unhealthy fruit.

- What does Jesus seem most concerned about in these verses in Matthew?

- How does he propose we get there?

PRACTICE

- Think about a movie or TV show you've seen where getting even is part of the plot—maybe it's a vendetta among characters, passive ways neighbors one-up one another, or maybe it's a violent retribution for a crime. What is your emotional response? (Are you cheering for one over the other, laughing, appalled?) Is this a satisfying response, do you think? Why or why not?

- Prayerfully take a minute to explore your own impulse to get even. Where have you experienced this impulse? What does it look like for you?

While the desire for justice is noble, enacting justice in practice is often difficult. Long before Mahatma (Mohandas) Gandhi said, "An eye for an eye makes the whole world blind," Jesus recognized that even just retaliation will tend to invite a counter-retaliation rather than peacefully resolving the situation. Jesus, therefore, invites his followers to be people who interrupt the cycle of retaliation, not with a decisive blow to their opponents but by absorbing the blow ourselves and offering mercy in return.

Jesus' desire for his people to go beyond justice and embody mercy goes against our natural impulse. Take a few minutes to consider the mercy you have received and how that could motivate you to show mercy to others.

DAY 2 LOVE YOUR ENEMIES

READ AND REFLECT

- **Start** with two minutes of silence.
- **Read Matthew 5:43-48.**

- **Write down** the imperative commands Jesus names in this section.

- **Go back** and **read Matthew 5:17-20**. If Jesus came not to abolish but to fulfill the law, what do you think he's doing in verses 43-48?

- How or why are Jesus' followers to do these things he outlines? See verse 45.

Embedded in the middle of this passage is the gospel motivation of verse 45: "So that you may be sons of your Father who is in heaven. For he makes his sun rise on the evil and on the good, and sends rain on the just and on the unjust." As Paul reminds us in Romans 5:10, it was "while we were enemies [that] we were reconciled to God by the death of his Son."

- Why does loving enemies make us sons of the Father?

- As an example of loving one's enemies, **READ GENESIS 50:20** about Joseph's reconciliation with his brothers who wanted him dead. What helped Joseph get to the point where he could bless his brothers?

As we think about what love asks of us, consider this illustration. On November 17, 1957, Dr. Martin Luther King Jr. preached a sermon on this passage at Dexter Avenue Baptist Church in Montgomery, Alabama. In his sermon, Dr. King told the following story about what had happened several years earlier when he and his brother were driving late at night on a dimly lit road in the South. Each driver they passed didn't dim their high beams:

> My brother A. D. looked over and in a tone of anger said: "I know what I'm going to do. The next car that comes along here and refuses to dim the lights, I'm going to fail to dim mine and pour them on in all of their power." And I looked at him right quick and said: "Oh no, don't do that. There'd be too much light on this highway, and it will end up in mutual destruction for all. Somebody got to have some sense on this highway."

> Somebody must have sense enough to dim the lights, and that is the trouble, isn't it? . . . Somebody must have sense enough and morality enough to cut off the chain of hate and the chain of evil in the universe. And you do that by love.

- From Dr. King's illustration, what does love require?

- How might loving our enemies be a way to keep the soil of our hearts less rocky and more healthy?

- If we don't love our enemies and instead retaliate, what grows in our hearts?

PRACTICE

Find a time today to share the story of Martin Luther King Jr. driving in the dark and passing discourteous drivers with a friend or family member.

- What are some ways in which you fail to "dim the lights"?

- What difference might it make if you interrupted the cycle of retaliation with love?

- **WRITE** a few sentences reflecting on your conversation and what you learned about yourself.

DAY 3 PRAY FOR YOUR ENEMIES

READ AND REFLECT

→ START with two minutes of silence.

→ READ MATTHEW 5:43-48.

We know how easy it is to ignore someone or walk away when you've been hurt by them, to effectively cut them off from you. It seems to hurt less that way. This is often what it looks like to deal with "enemies."

For Jesus' original audience in the first century, under Roman occupation, Rome was an enemy of the Jews. Gentiles could be considered enemies. Even those colluding with Rome, like tax collectors, were thought of as enemies. It seems natural to hate enemies and remove oneself from them.

- If you look up *enemy* in a dictionary, you'll see that the word comes from the Latin roots "not" and "friend." How does that change your understanding of who is an *enemy*?

- As you look over this passage, notice to whom this command is given. What difference does it make that it's given to a group of people about groups of people rather than to an individual?

- **Read** verses 45-47. What is the reasoning for Jesus' first audience (and us) to love our enemies?

- Frederick Dale Bruner writes that in loving our enemies we relate to God in an especially intimate way. We show we are his sons and daughters when we love our enemies. How do these commands reflect God's heart and how he desires to relate to us?

- If Jesus' followers loved and prayed for their enemies, what effect would this have on the larger society?

PRACTICE

It's possible to spend so much time unpacking this portion of Scripture that we never get around to actually praying. So, today we're shortening our daily devotion to actually *do* what Jesus says we must: pray for our enemies. Spend ten minutes praying for your enemies.

Jesus, you prayed for your own enemies on the cross. I name the enemies I have now before you. Those who have . . .

- ***wounded me or others (physically or emotionally) . . .***
- ***abandoned me . . .***
- ***forgotten me . . .***
- ***been unkind or unloving to me or others . . .***
- ***withheld approval . . .***
- ***withheld forgiveness . . .***

DAY 4 GIVING TO THE NEEDY

READ AND REFLECT

- **Start** with two minutes of silence.
- **Read Matthew 6:1-4.**

- Looking at verses 1 and 2, Jesus presumes his followers give to the needy but there are different motivations for them to do so. What are two different motivations Jesus mentions for giving or practicing righteousness in this passage?

- What does it mean to not let your left hand know what your right hand is doing?

- Why might this matter?

- What does Jesus promise for those who choose to keep their righteousness secret (v. 1)? Why do you think this matters?

Generosity isn't listed as a fruit of the Holy Spirit, yet the kindness and goodness mentioned in the list of the fruit of the Spirit in Galatians 5 often work themselves out in gratitude and cheerful giving. Spiritual fruit *can* be grown and cultivated (rather than simply growing because of a person's natural tendency).

SPIRITUAL FRUIT CAN BE GROWN AND CULTIVATED.

How does this happen? For one thing, spiritual fruit grows as we are close to Jesus. Robert Murray M'Cheyne, a nineteenth-century Scottish pastor, encouraged his congregation to grow in Christlikeness by giving generously, just as Jesus gave of himself. M'Cheyne motivated his congregation to generosity by responding to objections in a sermon:

> **Objection:** My money is my own.
>
> **Answer:** Christ might have said, "My blood is my own, my life is my own; no man forceth it from me." Then where should we have been? . . .
>
> Oh, my dear Christians! If you would be like Christ, give much, give often, give freely, to the vile and the poor, the thankless and the undeserving. Christ is glorious and happy, and so will you be. It is not your money I want, but your happiness. Remember his own word: "It is more blessed to give than to receive."

- Jesus says there is a reward for giving in secret (v. 4). What does this tell you about God's attention? How is the reward in verse 4 different from the rewards mentioned in verse 2?

- As you consider this passage, generosity that is the fruit of the Holy Spirit's work in our lives comes from reflecting on the generosity we have received from Christ. Where have you experienced the care and generosity of time and healing from Jesus in your own life?

- Remember spiritual fruit doesn't happen automatically! It's a process and God is patient as he grows fruit in us. As you look back, what evidence of growth in generosity do you see?

- **Read** Mark 5:21-43, looking at the stories of Jairus's daughter and the woman with a bleeding disorder. What do you notice about Jesus' lack of hurry and how he gives his undivided attention?

- What can you learn from that?

PRACTICE

- **READ 1 TIMOTHY 6:17-19**, Paul's first letter to his "child in the faith," Timothy. What might it look like to "set [your] hopes" on God and thank him for his rich provision? Spend some time in prayer, thanking God for his generosity to you.

- What is your default reaction when asked to give to the needy? In light of your prayerful reflection on this passage, how would you want to respond in the future when asked to give to the needy?

DAY 5 JESUS HAS SHOWN US MERCY

READ AND REFLECT

→ START with two minutes of silence.

Each week during the Day 5 lesson, we will spend some time meditating on the ways Jesus implements his teaching from the Sermon on the Mount and shows us what a fruitful life looks like.

→ READ MATTHEW 5:38–6:4.

In the Sermon on the Mount, Jesus is helping us connect the dots between what we believe about him and the way we live as his followers in the world. As Christians we believe that Jesus died to provide forgiveness for our sins, taking what we deserve—God's just punishment—on himself. But believing that Jesus died for our sins does not automatically make us people who are inclined to show mercy to others.

Becoming people who bear the fruit of the Holy Spirit's work in our lives is a process of repentance and faith. Fruitfulness always starts in the soil of repentance. Even when we don't see evidence of fruit, we can be confident that the Spirit will grow it in us.

We can start with repentance: we confess to God the specific ways in which we have failed God, and therefore need his mercy. And we continue in faith: we take hold of God's promises, believing that the good news God has offered to his people in general applies to us specifically. In faith we endeavor to live into the sort of life that Jesus calls us to, showing mercy to others even when it is hard to do so. In faith, we apply the promises of God to the specific areas we have repented of, laying hold of God's promises in the very place of our greatest need.

- **Write** and spend some time prayerfully journaling through this process of repentance and faith, using the Repentance and Faith table. First, use the left side of the table to write of what you can repent. Be specific. Where do you need God's mercy?

- When you have finished praying a prayer of repentance, use the right side of the table to write a prayer of faith for each item of repentance. (For example, if you desire to repent of gossip, you might pray for faith to be secure in who God says you are, so you don't need to resort to gossip). Finally, conclude this practice of repentance and faith with a prayer of gratitude, thanking God that Jesus lived a perfectly merciful life for you and is at work by his Spirit enabling you to show mercy to others.

PRACTICE

Take a ten-minute prayer walk today.

Before you begin your walk, think through this week's content and your own life circumstances. Where are you beginning to see the seriousness of God's law, and where are you finding it to be good?

How does following God's law lead to fruitfulness as a disciple? Remember that fruitfulness is looking more and more like Jesus and being characterized by the fruit of the Spirit.

In the first five minutes of your walk, practice prayers of repentance, and on your return, practice praying prayers of gratitude for God's mercy.

REPENTANCE AND FAITH

PRAYER OF REPENTANCE

PRAYER OF FAITH

PRAYER OF GRATITUDE

WEEK 4

FRUITFULNESS GROWS IN THE SOIL OF PRAYER

MATTHEW 6:5-15

GROUP SESSION

BEGIN

- **Start** with two minutes of silence.
- **Pray** and invite the Spirit to be present, shaping you as people as you discuss.
- **Opening Question:** How would you describe your attitude toward or experience of prayer?

READ

- **Read Matthew 6:5-15**

WATCH

- **Watch** video

DISCUSS

1. Are you tempted to use prayer, or some other religious activity, to appear to be good before others? What does that look like for you?
2. Jesus points out two ways we can use prayer hypocritically. His antidote to both is reminding us that God is our Father. How does your hypocrisy in prayer reveal your insecurity? How does remembering that God is your Father reshape this tendency?
3. Given that we all wonder at times whether our prayers make a difference, how might beginning your prayer by orienting your life around God and his glory affect your approach to prayer?
4. In the passage, what is our invitation to prayer? Who gives it and in what manner is it given?
5. How would it change your prayers if you approached God like a child running to their loving parent?

6. Think about this concept from Fleming Rutledge: when we pray "may your kingdom come" we are praying "may my kingdom go." In what ways are you prone to pray for your own kingdom? What would change about your prayers, or your life, if you began with God and his kingdom?

7. What does it mean, in your own words, to pray for God's kingdom to come?

8. One of the biggest challenges facing Christians today is that we tend to think God is there to help us feel better about ourselves. How does the Lord's Prayer challenge this assumption? What difference does that make in the way you approach your relationship with God?

9. Name one or two ways you'd like to see your own practice of prayer grow.

CLOSE

Remember that Jesus takes the pressure off.

Pray the Lord's Prayer together. Either pray it aloud in unison, or if you have time, use it as a template: after each line allow some moments of silence if anyone wants to add their own prayer as a response to the line just prayed.

DAY 1 THE GOD WHO IS HOLY AND CLOSE

READ AND REFLECT

- **Start** with two minutes of silence.
- **Read Matthew 6:5-15.**

Each day this week we'll reread the whole of the Lord's Prayer so it becomes a natural rhythm for this week's content.

- **Reread** verses 5-8. What does Jesus say characterizes hypocritical prayers?

- What are bad ways to pray, according to the passage?

- In verse 8, who invites us to pray? What sort of character does that person have?

It is revolutionary that the Lord's Prayer starts by addressing God as our Father. Here, we are invited as God's adopted sons and daughters into an intimate relationship with the Creator, who is perfect and powerful.

Verse 9 says we are to "hallow" God's name or to make it holy. If you look up the word *holy* in a dictionary, you'll find definitions that say something such as "set apart for religious purposes."

- What might it mean that we're invited to make God's name holy in prayer? What do you think this looks like?

If God is holy, he's also fully "other" than us. Though he is holy, God, our Father, doesn't stand far off. He invites us—because of the closeness we have through the Son—to call him the most intimate of names, "Abba" or "Daddy." Think about a beloved child calling her father "Daddy." How does she approach him with her words? With her body and time? What does she presume?

- Why would Jesus use the word *our* rather than *my* or *your* in verse 9?

- How does this corporate element fit with the privacy Jesus recommends in verse 6?

- **Reflect:** What does it mean for you today that your heavenly Father both invites you to call him Daddy and that he lacks nothing?

- How might this grow your confidence in how you approach him in prayer?

PRACTICE

To be holy isn't just about reverence, it's also about being whole. In some translations of Psalm 23:1, the second line, "I shall not want," is translated, "I have all that I need," or "I lack nothing." In God's presence we are increasingly being made whole. He cares for his people with the same care as a loving parent provides for, protects, and loves their children. In our practice today, we'll spend some more time connecting holiness and wholeness.

> IN GOD'S PRESENCE WE ARE INCREASINGLY BEING MADE WHOLE.

In the Old Testament, one of the leaders of God's people, Gideon, builds an altar and calls it Yahweh Shalom, The Lord Is Peace (Judges 6:24). Yet, *shalom* means more than our English word "peace" as a cessation of violence. Our prayers for the shalom of God focus on wholeness and completeness—that the way things are would be transformed into the way things should be.

- If God, rather than our circumstances, is our shalom—our completeness, our peace, and rest—take a minute to imagine what that would feel like in your body, in your family and friendships, in your neighborhood and place. Jot down a few notes.

Much of our modern Western world emphasizes wholeness as something we can attain through more hard work, more time off, or compassionate practices of care.

- If we presume that God is our shalom, what does that mean about the best way we might posture ourselves to attain wholeness?

- How does holiness connect to wholeness? We may think of holiness as legalistic rule following and doing churchy things. But if God is our Father, who has both the authority and the care to be gently present and powerful to correct wrongs, how does that change the way you see holiness?

READ 1 PETER 1:13-21, part of a letter addressed to persecuted Christians. Pay attention to where Peter writes that disciples are to be holy as God is holy.

- How does our status as adopted children enable our holy conduct?

Spend a few minutes in prayer. Look for an opportunity to share with a friend about connections you've made between holiness and wholeness.

DAY 2 YOUR KINGDOM COME

READ AND REFLECT

- **Start** with two minutes of silence.
- **Read Matthew 6:5-15.**

When Jesus was preaching and teaching, the Romans held absolute power over God's people, the Jews. Some Jews colluded with Rome for power and prestige. Others wanted to fight and overthrow their Roman oppressors. In this context, what might some of the original hearers have thought when they heard Jesus talking about a kingdom?

A kingdom isn't only a historical reality. Fleming Rutledge wrote in her book *Advent*: "If the kingdom of heaven is at hand, as John the Baptist says, then all our other kingdoms are called radically into question, including my own private kingdom, and yours." We may not be kings or queens, but we do still attempt to rule and reign over ourselves, our circumstances, and even over others.

Our own children sometimes imagine what it would be like to have unlimited resources or fame. But the impulse isn't just for kids! Have you ever thought that you have your own private kingdom? That you govern your own desires and dictate how all others should engage with you when entering your space? What is your kingdom like? What are its rules?

- Maybe you have strict rules about timeliness or cleanliness or lax edicts about having fun and not being tied down. Write out some rules of your kingdom. What are some characteristics of your kingdom?

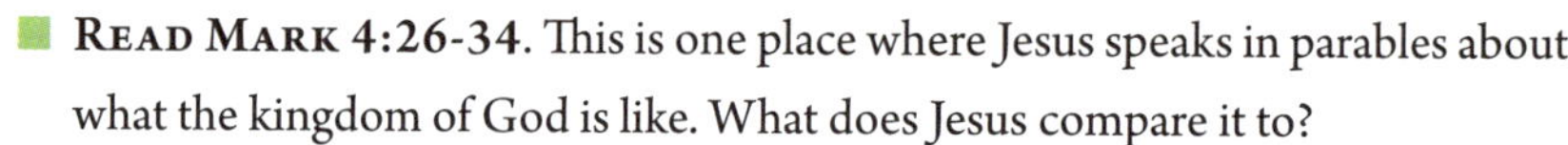

- **Read Mark 4:26-34.** This is one place where Jesus speaks in parables about what the kingdom of God is like. What does Jesus compare it to?

- Sometimes thinking about what metaphors Jesus doesn't use can help us get at what it ***is***. The kingdom isn't compared to a ship, an army, or even a family. What do these agricultural metaphors help us to understand about the kingdom of God?

- As we reflect on a fruitful life in which we look more and more like Jesus, considering these verses in Mark, how does fruitful growth (not unhealthy growth) happen in God's kingdom?

- Why is a mustard seed a helpful picture of God's kingdom? What does this tell us about the work of God (the Sower)?

- **Recall** what types of people are welcomed into God's kingdom in the Beatitudes. When we think about building a kingdom, we usually consider adding the best and brightest. How does Jesus' kingdom challenge the world's way of growing?

- What does it mean for God's kingdom to come on earth as it is in heaven? Does this request generally inform your own prayers?

PRACTICE

- **REFLECT:** Spend some time considering your own kingdom alongside God's kingdom.

- How does the abundant love of God reframe your kingdom? How does God's love challenge your own kingdom?

- On the image of a crown below, write down areas where you long for God's kingdom to come. On the outside of the image, write down what might need to be pruned or cut out of your life for God's kingdom to flourish.

- **PRAY:** Take some time to pray through this image.

- **APPLY:** What would it look like for God's kingdom in heaven to be carried out here on earth, and more specifically in your own home, neighborhood, and community? What would change?

- What small action might you practice to move forward into God's kingdom coming where you are, even this week?

DAY 3 OUR DAILY BREAD

READ AND REFLECT

- **START** with two minutes of silence.
- **READ MATTHEW 6:5-15.**

- **READ** the Lord's Prayer slowly. What sort of needs does the phrase "daily bread" (v. 11) imply?

Anne Lamott says there are basically three prayers: "Help," "Thanks," and "Wow." This verse in the Lord's Prayer is a "help" prayer. It presumes we have a good Father we can say "wow" to, so we can then come to God asking for our needs to be met.

- **READ LUKE 12:27-31.** In this passage of Scripture, Jesus speaks frankly about our need for tangible things like food, drink, and clothing. The impetus for such practical prayers comes from knowing that we have a Father who clothes the lilies of the fields and who won't neglect his children. How is asking for *daily* bread—today, and each day—different from asking for bread generally?

Part of the request for daily bread proceeds from relationship: children who are firm in God's love know that they are provided for and can ask daily for what they need. Consider this reality in the following application questions:

- When have you last asked for help—from a neighbor or from God? Do you relate to God more like a beloved child or are you trying to earn your keep? If the latter, what's holding you back?

- In your own requests, where might you have confused comfort with God's provision? What's the difference?

- What are your needs, your daily bread, that you may not have brought to God? What about the needs of your neighborhood, city, church, or community?

- We are so used to providing for our own needs. Even as you take responsibility for yourself and your community, how do you (or could you) display this posture of confident request?

- **Read** verse 12 of the Lord's Prayer. As you consider the next line of the prayer: "forgive us our debts, as we also have forgiven our debtors," how does this relate to asking God for our daily bread? Is forgiveness a need? How might this logically follow the request for our daily bread?

- Do you tend to think of your need for forgiveness as part of your need for daily sustenance from God?

- As we consider this confident request for daily bread, what does this teach us about a fruitful life?

PRACTICE

We can tend to think of fruitfulness as all the things we do. In planting a vegetable garden, we purchase seeds, we prepare the soil, we work on compost, we dig holes, we water and fertilize the soil. But ultimately, we don't make anything grow at all. When conditions are right, healthy growth happens!

- In what ways do you both ***do*** many things and also do nothing in your own spiritual life?

For the rest of the week, practice praying the Lord's Prayer at a specific time of day. This is both an action we do and something to receive from God. Daily prayer is something we can commit to and do, but it is God who grows fruit from any spiritual habit.

As you pray the Lord's Prayer each day, change your posture, such as choosing to kneel during your lunch break. Or recite it around the family dinner table. At the end of the week, notice how this has informed your days, your prayers, and your view of God as Father. Write down where and when you plan to pray, and come back to this spot in a week to journal about the effects of your daily prayer. Take a moment to journal about this effect.

DAY 4 FORGIVE US OUR SINS

READ AND REFLECT

- **START** with two minutes of silence.
- **READ MATTHEW 6:5-15.**

We often desire mercy for ourselves and justice for everyone else. Asking the Father to "forgive us as we forgive others" is stark indeed. In each section of the Sermon on the Mount, Jesus never lets us fall into abstractions. We can't love God apart from loving our neighbor. We can't expect forgiveness from God when we withhold it from others. Doing so would be putting ourselves, not God, on the throne of judgment.

- **READ PSALM 103:10-14**, a passage written about a thousand years before Christ. In this passage, what, on God's part, prompts God's forgiveness?

- Who receives God's forgiveness?

- What is your response to this mercy?

- **Take a moment:** What is the state of your forgiveness toward others? Are you nursing a grudge or afraid to give up what power you hold by withholding forgiveness?

Forgiving does not mean an excuse for wrongdoing, nor does it mean a lack of consequences. Instead, when we practice forgiving others as an act of will and love for God, we finally entrust the one who has wronged us to both the mercy and judgment of God. Only God rules with equity. Vengeance is his, not ours.

> WHEN WE PRACTICE FORGIVING OTHERS, WE FINALLY ENTRUST THE ONE WHO HAS WRONGED US TO BOTH THE MERCY AND JUDGMENT OF GOD.

- For what do you need to forgive someone else? Of what do you need to repent?

The Lord's Prayer is also communal. We are to pray for *our* sins to be forgiven. If we grew up in the West, it's nearly impossible to think about collective guilt or sin. It is likewise hard to not interpret all of the Sermon on the Mount, and the Lord's Prayer specifically, through the lens of *me* alone.

- Yet, what do we (a communal *we*) need to repent of? Maybe it's something unique to your place or community or something more general like enthrallment to politics to functionally save you. Maybe it's something in your generational or national past. Write down some possibilities for corporate repentance.

- Why does it matter that prayer to God be to ***our*** Father and to forgive us ***our*** sins? In what ways have you privatized your growth in grace to be only individual, intellectual, or emotional, and disconnected from a people and a place?

PRACTICE

PRAY in company with the Spirit, allowing the Spirit to bring up any unhealed wounds from your lack of forgiveness.

PRACTICE opening your hands as a bodily release of a person (maybe even yourself) or an event that causes a shadow to hang on your past. Feel free to jot down some thoughts from this prayer practice.

Now, given that the fruitful Christian life is not something done individually, choose one thing from your prayer time and share with a group member or other friend.

DAY 5 JESUS PRODUCES FRUIT IN YOU

READ AND REFLECT

➜ START with two minutes of silence.

Each week during the Day 5 lesson, we will spend some time meditating on the ways Jesus implements his teaching from the Sermon on the Mount and shows us what a fruitful life looks like.

As we work our way through the Lord's Prayer, we see how Jesus himself followed these movements of prayer. He was often found getting up and going off to pray in the dark of the night. He prioritized prayer and time spent in the presence of his Father. As we consider the lines of the Lord's Prayer, we'll consider some moments in Jesus' life where he lived out this prayer:

Our Father in heaven, hallowed be your name. Jesus called God Father. All that Jesus does proceeds from his love for and obedience to the Father.

Your kingdom come, your will be done, on earth as it is in heaven. In the Garden of Gethsemane, Jesus actively submits his will to the will of the Father in the plan that the triune God made before the beginning of time to rescue and redeem the world through the sacrifice of Jesus.

Give us this day our daily bread, and forgive us our debts, as we also have forgiven our debtors. And lead us not into temptation, but deliver us from evil. He broke the loaves and prayed the Father would multiply them to meet the daily needs of Jesus' followers. He was actually led by the Spirit into his temptations in the wilderness and there Jesus told Satan that he had a sustenance through the Word of God that Satan couldn't comprehend. He trusted the Father for his daily needs.

For yours is the kingdom, the power, and the glory, forever and ever. Amen. All of Jesus' life was lived in reverence to the Father to be the self-giving shalom come into the world to make us and all of creation right with God. Through his death and resurrection, Jesus conquers death itself, ransoming us to real, kingdom life. In his ascension, he still prays—he intercedes for us at the right hand of the Father.

Jesus lived the Lord's Prayer.

PRACTICE

Today, we'll spend some time considering one line of the Lord's Prayer, "Give us this day our daily bread." Let's look at a well-known miracle of Jesus, the feeding of the five thousand.

- **READ MATTHEW 14:13-21.** What do you learn about Jesus from this passage?

- What do you learn about the Father?

- What do you learn about God's heart toward people?

- What will you do in response?

If this has been a helpful practice, consider spending more time in a passage of Scripture where Jesus exemplifies part of living out the Lord's Prayer, such as: the healing of a paralytic (Matthew 9:1-8), Jesus' temptations in the wilderness (Matthew 4:1-11), Jesus praying for believers (John 17:20-26), and the passion in the Garden of Gethsemane (Matthew 26:36-46).

Use the questions in this box to help remind you that fruitfulness always flows from Christ. What are you learning about how growth happens in a disciple's life? In the life cycle of a seed—from planting, to underground germination, to first sprouts, to stability and then pruning, or letting the ground lie fallow between growth cycles—where do you find yourself now?

WEEK 5

PRUNING SO THAT YOU MAY BEAR FRUIT

MATTHEW 6:16-34

GROUP SESSION

BEGIN

- **Start** with two minutes of silence.
- **Pray** and invite the Spirit to be present, shaping you as people as you discuss.
- **Opening question:** How has the Lord's Prayer reshaped your praying this last week?

READ

- **Read Matthew 6:16-34**

WATCH

- **Watch** video

DISCUSS

1. How has a spiritual discipline or practice been helpful to you in the past?
2. Have you ever fasted before? What was that experience like?
3. There are several mentions in this section about our treasure and reward. Looking at the passage, how would you summarize Jesus' approach to these words?
4. How does your financial budget illustrate your priorities, and how might it show the fruit of your spiritual life?
5. How would you state verse 25 in your own words? How does this relate to the cost of fruitfulness?
6. In what ways might practicing spiritual disciplines be a way to use God for his gifts rather than as a way to connect with God?
7. As you look to the week ahead, what things, people, or events come to mind that would cause you to worry? What do you dream about?
8. Consider writing down a list of your current worries and anxieties. Imagine what it would feel like to experience God's care around each worry, knowing that each is held. Confess

ways you've used religious activity to try to get rid of your worries or look for a circumstantial solution to an issue of faith.

9. What is the function of the "therefore" in verse 25?

10. As you think about how spiritual growth happens underground and out of sight, what can you conclude about some of these out-of-sight places like finances and worry? Can God meet you even there?

11. Reflect together about the spiritual practice of silence with God and with each other these last few weeks. How has this felt like pruning? What fruit has resulted from this daily practice of silence with God?

CLOSE

- **Remember** that Jesus takes the pressure off.
- **Pray** in small groups. Consider sharing some of your worries together.

DAY 1 FASTING

READ AND REFLECT

→ **Start** with two minutes of silence.

In another Gospel, Mark writes:

> Now John's disciples and the Pharisees were fasting. And people came and said to him, "Why do John's disciples and the disciples of the Pharisees fast, but your disciples do not fast?" And Jesus said to them, "Can the wedding guests fast while the bridegroom is with them? As long as they have the bridegroom with them, they cannot fast. The days will come when the bridegroom is taken away from them, and then they will fast in that day." (Mark 2:18-20)

- From this passage in Mark, what does Jesus say is the reason his followers would fast?

Read Matthew 6:16-18. The "when you fast" opening presupposes that Jesus' disciples will and do fast. Fasting, then, is a spiritual discipline that many religious people could use to gain acclaim or respect from others. But Jesus talks about fasting as a way to mourn his absence and is tied here only to the reward and acclaim of God.

- Do you know of anyone with a fasting practice? Why do they fast?

- Why, do you think, Jesus draws attention to fasting's hiddenness? Why is this important?

We can easily get hung up about the specifics of fasting and think, as we did, that fasting was for super Christians. How long and how often should we fast? What might a fast look like? Yet, given what we've read already in Jesus' sermon, these words are likely less to do with the details of fasting and more to do with *how* we go about doing religious things. Jesus seems to be concerned more about the hearts of his followers—not showing off their works or deeds, looking "gloomy like the hypocrites" (v. 16)—than he does about the specifics of a practice.

- There's a larger question here. What do we imagine our reward to be for our practices? Why do we do "Christian" things?

- What is our motivation for going to church, praying, and reading Scripture? If we're honest, do we even do these things regularly? Do we go to church, read the Bible, fast, or pray because we love God, or because we think it pleases God, or because we want people to think of us as good, moral people?

- If fasting is a practice to mourn God's absence, how might fasting bring you closer to God?

Historically, many Christians have practiced seasons of fasting around the liturgical church calendar, particularly during Advent or Lent. We know that we cannot always feast (in body or soul), but rhythms of fasting and feasting are both necessary. They prime our spiritual muscles to receive from God in gratitude in plenty and to fall upon his grace and mercy when we fast. Jesus links fasting (and spiritual disciplines more generally) with connection to God the Father and here, to reward.

- To what extent is love of God treasure enough?

PRACTICE

This week choose a period of time to fast from something—whether it's from food, a TV show, shopping, or another way you reward yourself.

- **What will you fast from?**

The period of time you try fasting needs to be long enough for you to notice its absence.

■ **WRITE DOWN** the period of time and what day(s) you'll fast from this thing.

Don't tell others you're fasting and go about your day. During this time, practice praying the Lord's Prayer when your stomach rumbles or when you want to sit in comfort with that new Netflix drama. After you've completed your fast, use the following journaling prompts to reflect:

- I notice when I practice fasting, I generally unthinkingly turn to __________ in order to escape/distract/numb (or something else). . . .
- I notice I don't have rhythms of fasting or feasting and this makes me think . . .
- Instead of turning to X, I tried an alternate practice of Y and noticed. . . .
- Thinking about God himself as my treasure, makes me consider . . .
- When I think of a fruitful Christian life, I realize that fasting is like pruning and . . .

DAY 2 HEAVENLY TREASURE

READ AND REFLECT

- **Start** with two minutes of silence.
- **Read Matthew 6:19-24.**

The Christian life isn't cordoned off from how we spend our days, as if prayer and fasting were closet spiritual experiences that have no bearing on how we live or earn a living. Faith in Jesus *does* look like aiming for an audience of One (for God himself versus human approval), but it's not separated from our bodies or our bank accounts.

As we considered in the group lesson, this section of Jesus' sermon connects the kingdom of God to the ways we seek ultimate meaning, value, purpose, and security. And a kingdom life changes how we relate to money.

- What sort of attitude about money did you grow up with? Was there never enough, too much, or not quite enough?

Most of us think that if we had just a little bit more money we'd be okay. So we end up serving our bank accounts by caring too much or too little, by lacking generosity in our penny-pinching or in our extravagance. But money isn't just something to manage, it's a spiritual power.

- Jesus makes the connection between money and bodily health. Look at verses 22-23. How would you describe a healthy, fruitful way of dealing with money?

- Verse 24 might surprise you with its directness. What could serving money look like?

The King James Version translation of Matthew 6:24 doesn't use the word *money*, but instead keeps "mammon" from Aramaic: "Ye cannot serve God and mammon." Andy Crouch writes about the pervasive and demonic hold money has in *The Life We're Looking For*: "By the first centuries of the Christian church, teachers and bishops had concluded that in using the name Mammon, Jesus had in mind not just a concept but a demonic power. Money, for Jesus, was not a neutral tool but something that could master a person every bit as completely as the true God."

- How have you seen the mastering power of Mammon at work? Where has it been at work in you? In your church and community?

It's not just dollars or bitcoin. Crouch talks about mammon as an "anti-God impetus that finds its power in money." Money sells. Money talks. Money promises a limitless and all-powerful existence, devoid of responsibility to anyone or anything that we do not choose.

- Where have you seen your desire for what money promises grow too large?

- If it's not a number that you desire, what is underneath your desire for more (such as approval, a sense of stability, being a part of a particular neighborhood, or having more control)?

- We cannot serve both God and money. What do our daydreams about prosperity, our constant checking of our balances, or our worries reveal about where we place our treasure?

PRACTICE

- **LOOK** through your transaction history and bank account. **NOTICE** your spending, saving, and giving patterns. What do you notice?

In the Old Testament especially, the idea of giving your firstfruits—the best fruit of the vine, the unblemished animal—to God was paramount to being a wholehearted, fruitful member of God's covenant people.

> GIVING YOUR FIRSTFRUITS TO GOD WAS PARAMOUNT TO BEING A WHOLEHEARTED, FRUITFUL MEMBER OF GOD'S COVENANT PEOPLE.

- As you look at your income, where do your firstfruits go?

- The Scripture is stark: you cannot serve both God and money. What has your review of your finances revealed? What are some opportunities for you to use your money for God's kingdom?

PRAY about your financial needs, desires, plans, and the kingdom of God.

DAY 3 ANXIETY

READ AND REFLECT

- **Start** with two minutes of silence.
- **Read Matthew 6:25-34.**

■ **Reread** verses 25-27. What is your first reaction to Jesus' command to not worry? Does this seem possible to you? Why or why not?

■ What would need to happen for you to not be anxious about anything?

OUR COMMON HUMAN EXPERIENCE OF ANXIETY IS OFTEN THE RESULT OF OUR DOUBLE LIVES, LIVING DIVIDED BETWEEN THE WORLD'S STATUS-SEEKING AND LIVING AS CHILDREN OF GOD.

Our common human experience of anxiety is often the result of our double lives—when we are divided between the world's status-seeking and living as children of God in his kingdom of grace and surprising mercy. Or, as we consider our double lives using the metaphor of fruitfulness, it's as if we're plants with shallow roots and wondering why we keep falling over when the winds blow.

It is impossible to serve and love God while angling for comfort, success, prestige, or renown. The kingdom of God is not simply a set of assertions about reality or the end of time, but it is an all-encompassing cosmos that envelops and reorders reality. And it comes with a price—but it's the only place where real joy and contentment grow.

- What keeps you up at night? Where does your anxiety creep in?

When we aim our lives toward the approval of God, where he is our audience of one, we will no longer be ruled by what we think money can get us. In these verses Jesus brings up sources of our anxieties: clothing, food, drink—the real realities of being able to live in the world.

Can we simply not be anxious? This may seem impossible or legalistic. But this lack of ultimate fear and worry is the physical and spiritual result of faith, of inhabiting a peace that passes understanding. Reading Jesus' commands in Matthew 6, and as we realize how deeply we fall short, we're thrown back to the Beatitudes as we come again to our own spiritual poverty and the covenant faithfulness of God. We feel our poverty of spirit, our meekness, and we begin to really hunger for a life characterized by mercy and to be those who hunger and thirst after righteousness.

- **Reread** the Beatitudes in Matthew 5. What stands out to you now?

In this passage in chapter 6, Jesus commends the lilies and grass of the field and the birds of the air as part of God's created order that he lovingly clothes and provides for.

- How does the natural world testify to the goodness of God?

- Where do you desire to be freed from worry, anxiety, fear, control, or the false promises of more? Name those in prayer.

PRACTICE

Take a short ten-minute prayer walk around your neighborhood and notice the natural world. Pay attention to trees, grasses, birds, worms, and flowers. How do you see God providing for the created order? Reflect with God about his provision, your own hustle, and pray for faith to trust him.

After your walk, if you'd like, journal about God's care for creation you saw on your walk.

DAY 4 ANXIOUS ABOUT THE FUTURE

READ AND REFLECT

- **Start** with two minutes of silence.
- **Read Matthew 6:25-34.**

Much of our anxiety concerns the future—we don't know how political leaders or the economy might affect our work or our security. We're unsure about health or a strained relationship. We don't know about the world our children or grandchildren will inherit. So to combat our fear we can often turn to planning, cynicism, exhaustion, or a devil-may-care attitude.

- What are some of your reactions to the unknowns of the future? Do you plan, scheme, detach, or choose cynicism?

- Why does Jesus use the examples of birds and flowers? How might these examples ease your own anxieties?

- Who are the pagans or Gentiles Jesus is referring to here? How are Jesus' followers to be different from them (like salt and light in Matthew 5)?

Jesus tells his hearers: your heavenly Father knows that you need clothes, food, and a place to lay your head (Matthew 6:32). When we are like those who "earnestly seek after" these things, we spin our wheels. When we trust God to ultimately meet our needs, we stay in the present.

- Are you more oriented to the past, present, or future in how you spend your time thinking?

Jesus reminds us: "Sufficient for the day is its own trouble" or "Each day has enough trouble of its own," (Matthew 6:34 ESV and NIV). You do not know how the past will affect the future, nor do you know what is coming. All we have is today. This doesn't mean that we don't plan or have goals, but it does mean that we can't "borrow trouble" (as Ashley's grandmother used to say).

- What trouble are you borrowing? Make a list below.

PRACTICE

Today, we'll spend some time in other parts of Scripture to help us with the themes contained in Matthew 6:25-34.

In Jesus' parable of the sower, Jesus describes seed being choked by weeds. When he explains the parable later to his disciples, Jesus says: "As for what was sown among thorns, this is the one who hears the word, but the cares of the world and the deceitfulness of riches choke the word, and it proves unfruitful. As for what was sown on good soil, this is the one who hears the word and understands it. He indeed bears fruit and yields, in one case a hundredfold, in another sixty, and in another thirty" (Matthew 13:22-23).

- In these two verses, circle that which prohibits the fruitful kingdom growth in a person. Underline in the passage what the difference is between the seed that grows and is fruitful and the one that dies.

- What are some of your conclusions about fruitfulness?

READ GENESIS 1:1-2: "In the beginning, God created the heavens and the earth. The earth was without form and void, and darkness was over the face of the deep. And the Spirit of God was hovering over the waters."

And Genesis 2:8-9: "And the LORD God planted a garden in Eden, in the east, and there he put the man whom he had formed. And out of the ground the LORD God made to spring up every tree that is pleasant to the sight and good for food."

- In these first verses of the Bible, what do you notice about the goodness of creation? What do you notice about God's care for creation?

- Given what you've noticed in Scripture, spend some time praying: name both God's care for creation along with your own anxieties and what you're learning about fruitfulness.

DAY 5 JESUS IS OUR TREASURE

READ AND REFLECT

→ START with two minutes of silence.

Each week during the Day 5 lesson, we will spend some time meditating on the ways Jesus implements his teaching from the Sermon on the Mount and shows us what a fruitful life looks like.

Jesus was financially dependent on others in his ministry of teaching and healing. He sent out his disciples and told them not to take extra clothing. Just a few chapters after the Sermon on the Mount, Jesus mentions that following him will be costly: "Foxes have holes, and birds of the air have nests, but the Son of Man has nowhere to lay his head" (Matthew 8:20).

Even though we may not be physically poor or homeless, as believers in Jesus we will not fit in. We will not fit the world's standards of success. We may be passed over on account of our faith in Christ.

Jesus was poor. He was homeless. He knew that following him would carry a cost. Kingdom life is about downward, not upward, mobility. READ JOHN 15:18: "If the world hates you, know that it has hated me before it hated you."

- How does this verse speak about the cost of discipleship?

- How much does this fit your own life experience? If it doesn't, why do you think that is?

The second person of the Trinity left heavenly riches not only to take on our human flesh with its limits, but more than that, to become poor and needy. Those of us with homes, money in the bank, and an education rely on these things for our sustenance more than our faith in God. When we know our need and our poverty of spirit, we must throw ourselves on the mercy of God.

- Think about what it might look like in your life if Jesus were your ultimate treasure: what you prized above all else.

- What would you let go of? What would you be freed from? List some things here.

When we, through the power of the Spirit, spend our lives singly and secretly loving God and our neighbor, we will be freed from the need for approval, fortune, renown, respectability, or power. We will be free to be ourselves and freed to actually do good in the world.

> **WE ARE TO TAKE HEART BECAUSE JESUS HAS ALREADY AND WILL FULLY OVERCOME DEATH AND THE POWERS OF DEATH ITSELF, INCLUDING MAMMON.**

Jesus says: "In the world you will have tribulation. But take heart; I have overcome the world" (John 16:33). He does not say to take heart because of a good plan, or right doctrine, or to work it out through worry. We are to take heart because Jesus has already and will fully overcome death and the powers of death itself, including mammon. It is Jesus giving himself up for us that makes us right before God. Ultimately, trouble that comes can't touch us because, in Christ, all our needs are met! What hope that brings us as we are worried about many things.

PRACTICE

- How might God be calling you to act in light of this truth? Use the following for a prompt for prayer and journaling: God, you know the things that clutter my mind and weigh down my heart . . .

PRAY by naming or drawing the things that weigh you down with anxiety, and then draw a larger picture of a cross as a visual reminder that God's love in Christ covers our fears, insecurities, and more than makes up for the cost of following Jesus.

WEEK 6

FRUITFULNESS IS NOT A SPECTATOR SPORT

MATTHEW 7:1-11

GROUP SESSION

BEGIN

- **Start** with two minutes of silence.
- **Pray** and invite the Spirit to be present, shaping you as people as you discuss.
- **Opening Question:** Where do you notice a disconnect between Jesus' words and life and your own words and life? What is your hope going forward?

READ

- **Read Matthew 7:1-11**

WATCH

- **Watch** video

DISCUSS

1. How is judgment a spectator sport in the media? Where have you seen news organizations focus on judgment rather than constructive action?
2. How might you know if judgment is appropriate or not? When have people given you the opportunity to offer discernment in their lives?
3. As you read the passage together, what sort of judgment is Jesus talking about here?
4. When have you experienced someone who had something challenging to say to you, but they did so without you feeling shamed or ostracized?
5. It's easy to call our judgments of another person or group "discernment"—so we equate our preferences as the standard for "good" or "right" behavior without considering a different preference or context. To what extent are your judgments or discernments actually condemnations of another person? Or when have you been condemned by someone's "discernment"? Provide examples.

6. How could verses 1-6 (on judgment) and 7-11 (on asking of God) relate?
7. Dallas Willard writes that this passage on judgment comes after Jesus' disciples have reckoned with anger, contempt, and lusting. These may be the logs in our collective eyes. Only then can we offer discernment that might help another person. What is your response to this important order?
8. What does verse 6 mean, do you think? How does it relate to the communal nature of spiritual growth?
9. When there's fear and anxiety in a system, it's easy to rush to advice-giving and judgment. What actions are necessary in your own life to avoid this reaction?
10. What area in your life might you want to focus on giving love and lessening your anger or contempt? If you're willing to share, is there a person or people you'd like to begin to let go of condemning?
11. What are you learning more generally about the fruitful life of following Jesus? Are you looking more like Jesus, living as he did and loving as he did?

CLOSE

→ **Remember** that Jesus takes the pressure off.

Pray: In smaller groups, spend some time praying together, entrusting others in your family, neighborhood, church, or work environments to God rather than using judgment to manipulate and condemn.

DAY 1 DON'T JUDGE

READ AND REFLECT

- **START** with two minutes of silence.
- **READ MATTHEW 7:1-5.**

Jesus is interested not in theoretical disciples but in ones who bear real fruit in their lived experiences. As with issues of lust, divorce, oaths, anxiety, or money, this section on judgment is immensely practical.

Frederick Dale Bruner writes in his commentary that this section is the fifth Beatitude in reverse.

- **REREAD** Matthew 5:7. What is the motivation in Matthew 5:7 for Jesus' disciples to follow him? How about in 7:1-5?

- How are mercy and judgment related?

When we judge ourselves, we tend to look at ourselves more favorably than others. We're often blind to our own sinful patterns or the patterns and systems of our group (whether that's a church, place, family, or nation).

- What corporate or collective judgment have you observed or been a part of?

- In verse 5, the word *hypocrite* is used again. Prayer was a place where hypocrisy could be present according to Jesus. How is hypocrisy a temptation in this situation?

- As you look at verses 3-5, how is a community necessary for Christian fruitfulness? In what ways might we hinder transformation in another?

- How might we help transformation progress?

PRACTICE

Today we're going to practice praying through Scripture. Rather than stew in our past, we will be bringing the topic of judgment to God in prayer. Here are steps of lectio divina, a way of interacting with Scripture as we listen for God's voice and practice being in his presence.

Begin in silence in God's presence. Ask the Spirit to be present as you read God's Word and apply it. Breathe in and out. Then, after a few minutes, slowly **READ MATTHEW 7:1-5** out loud.

READ the passage a second time, this time more slowly than the first. Is there a word or phrase that speaks to you?

Holding that phrase or word in your mind, let that word or phrase interact with your thoughts, experiences, or feelings. What does this bring up for you? Is there a new insight, a sense of God's nearness, or something to repent of, as you consider this phrase in Scripture? Sit with these questions.

READ through the passage a third time. As you think about this passage and your own experiences, use this time to respond to God in prayer. Tell him how this passage hits you today.

READ through the passage a fourth time. Simply rest in God's presence. There is nothing you need to do—no insight or plan to make happen right now. Feel the pleasure of God.

DAY 2 BUT SHOW CARE

READ AND REFLECT

- **Start** with two minutes of silence.
- **Read Matthew 7:1-6.**

When we read verse 6 about not giving pearls to pigs or giving dogs holy things, we can tend to think that this verse is about discerning who is worth our goodness or the gospel's goodness before we share something. Dallas Willard reminds us that for pigs, pearls are indigestible. Holy things—like a Bible—are simply unusable to dogs.

- Based on verse 6, why is it unwise to place precious things in front of those who cannot appreciate them?

When we consider the Sermon on the Mount as a whole, we must start as Christians by first addressing the needs of the body. As many of us may know from experience, for children who are hungry or tired, these bodily needs must be met before we ask them to clean up their room. If we desire to share the goodness of Jesus with a neighbor, we don't start with condemnation; we start with a dinner invitation. We start with friendship and caring for others before we share holy things. We start with things that are useful, age-appropriate, and digestible.

> **IF WE DESIRE TO SHARE THE GOOD NEWS OF JESUS WITH A NEIGHBOR, WE START WITH A DINNER INVITATION.**

- How have you or someone you knew started too deep too quickly when speaking of matters of faith?

- When has judgment clouded your view of another person? Write down some details.

- **Think** about how you might share your gospel hope with someone. What would be age-appropriate as well as appropriate for that person's context?

- As you consider a specific person, how could allowing for maturity or context be useful? What sorts of ideas, concepts, or emotions might be able to be grasped, or made digestible, with this person?

- What is the connection between judgment, care, and growing into a fruitful Christian?

PRACTICE

In Rembrandt's painting *The Return of the Prodigal Son*, we see the moment when the prodigal is welcomed back into the embrace of the father. (The parable is told in Luke 15:11-32.) The prodigal son in Jesus' parable had more than he needed and literally squandered all that he had. He was reduced to caring for pigs and eating their slop. We see that the father welcomed him back not with condemnation but with grace.

OBSERVE Rembrandt's painting on the next page. The story of the prodigal son that Jesus told involves a faithful father welcoming both his proud son who stayed home and the wasteful son who ran away and then came back ruined but repentant.

- **REFLECT** on the artwork. What do you notice? What is the father's embrace like? Who do you have questions about in the painting? What thoughts, experiences, or ideas come to mind as you sit with the painting?

- How do you think Matthew 7:6 relates to Jesus' teaching on judgment in Matthew 7:1-5? As we think about the idea of judgment, what thoughts or emotions does this painting bring up for you?

Now spend some time with God in prayer. Tell him about your response to this painting. Is there something it brings up that you want to address with him? Perhaps it leads you to gratitude, repentance, or an act of generosity and service. Write down your reflections.

DAY 3 ASK, SEEK, AND KNOCK

READ AND REFLECT

- **START** with two minutes of silence.
- **READ MATTHEW 7:7-11.**

These verses are astounding: "Ask, and it will be given to you; seek, and you will find; knock, and it will be opened to you." We can often be too glib with God, viewing him as a cosmic genie who will grant our wishes. We can also be so afraid of asking God incorrectly or imperfectly that instead, we act as if we're frightened children who are fearful of a parent's negative response and so do not ask.

Jesus tells us to ask, seek, and knock. These are action verbs. To ask is to petition; it involves a posture of humility and a sense that our asking actually matters and it will be heard. Seeking means we are active participants, not simply waiting around to see what happens. Knocking implies that we move toward people, callings, and options, and test them out to see what happens.

- **READ** verse 8. Is it saying we get whatever we ask for? Why or why not?

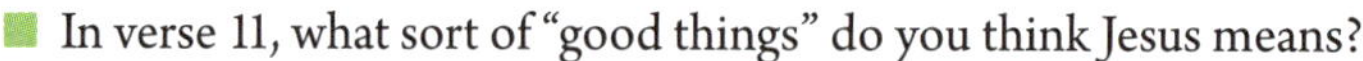

- In verse 11, what sort of "good things" do you think Jesus means?

In these verses, Jesus presupposes a good Father who cares for and responds to his children.

- What is your attitude toward God in prayer? Are you too timid or overly familiar?

- What might be the invitation here from Jesus about how you relate to God in prayer? Write down a few thoughts.

- Where have you seen God's goodness in your past? Or God's goodness for someone else, your place, or your community? Write down these markers of remembrance below.

Several times in the Old Testament, God's people would build something as a visual reminder of God's care and faithfulness—an *ebenezer*, meaning a "stone of help." It wasn't superstition, but it was a reminder that we often need something tangible to remind us of God's care because we so easily forget. As you pray below, perhaps light a candle or hold a stone as a tangible reminder of God's care. Come to God as a child with your desires.

PRACTICE

In your prayer time today practice moving your body into a state of asking. Maybe kneel down, go for a walk, or raise your hands. Put your body in a state of expectancy.

- ***Asking:*** Instead of worrying or even using our anxieties to fuel condemnation of others, what might you instead ask God about?

- ***Seeking:*** Instead of adding more information or planning now, practice seeking God's guidance and care concerning the things you're asking him about. Write your prayer.

- ***Knocking:*** What might be a next step to take in your life concerning the things that cloud your head and keep you up at night?

DAY 4 THE GOODNESS OF THE FATHER

READ AND REFLECT

- **START** with two minutes of silence.
- **READ MATTHEW 7:7-11.**

- When have you enjoyed giving a gift to someone? What was it and what made you excited to give it?

We wouldn't give those we love things that harm them or do not meet their very real needs. Here, Jesus reminds us that we have a good Father, full of absolute perfect goodness.

- Do you believe God is withholding what you need or desire? In what areas of your life are you choosing to not really ask, seek, or knock at God's door? Why?

Have you been in the presence of an older Christian who has weathered hardship, suffering, or unfulfilled desires and yet radiates joy and contentment? Part of this is a resilience that's built not just on their skills but on a belief in the goodness of God to lead them through places of discomfort, pain, and suffering—all for their good and God's glory.

Resilience is a muscle that can be strengthened through practice; it's not just something some of us are born with and others aren't. One of the ways we grow more resilient is through concrete action, rather than always reacting. Resilience also grows within a supportive community. It's hard to be resilient on your own. Resilience grows through seeing that hardships and setbacks are not the end of the story.

> **RESILIENCE GROWS THROUGH SEEING THAT HARDSHIPS AND SETBACKS ARE NOT THE END OF THE STORY.**

Resilience ultimately grows when you are in a resilient community, when you are confident that you have purpose and are heard by God, that he is in charge, and that he is kind and good.

If you'd like a visual picture, you can think of resilience as the hearty tomato plant that is connected to a trellis. With support and the right conditions, it bears fruit. Conversely, a plant without support easily falls away and certainly bears less fruit than it could.

Take a few minutes to notice things in your own life that add to or take away from your resilience as a follower of Jesus.

- Things that contribute to a resilient posture:

- Things that detract from a resilient posture:

PRACTICE

NOTICE in your body where you tend to feel worry and anxiety. Does your stomach get tied in knots or do your shoulders lift up? How have you used worry or anxiety to put a pause on your growth in resilience?

At several points throughout your day, stop and do a body scan, maybe before meals or at bedtime. Spend a few moments paying attention to how your body feels from your head to your toes. Notice any places of discomfort. Notice if something is tight or out of whack. As you pay attention to each part of your body, pray to your good Father: thank him for his kindness, thank him for each body part, and practice entrusting yourself fully to his care. Take note of what you notice.

Then, finish your day in prayer, using the following prompts to guide you:

- What has God given you for which you can thank him?

- What specifically can you ask him for?

- What would it look like for you to relax, knowing that he cares for you?

DAY 5 JESUS ASKS, WE RECEIVE

READ AND REFLECT

→ **Start** with two minutes of silence.

Each week during the Day 5 lesson, we will spend some time meditating on the ways Jesus implements his teaching from the Sermon on the Mount and shows us what a fruitful life looks like.

→ **Read Matthew 7:1-11.**

Read Luke 11:5-8, a story Jesus tells about a persistent friend who comes asking for bread at midnight. It's not *care* that makes the man inside answer the door and give him bread but the friend's impudence. Jesus tells this parable to remind his followers that we can ask and even demand from God—not because we are trying to manipulate God but because we are so needy.

- How do you tend to approach God in prayer? How might Jesus' teaching on prayer in Luke 11 give you permission to pray differently?

Throughout his life, Jesus models asking liberally of his Father. He sneaks off to pray in the middle of the night. He petitions his Father to heal and to feed those who are needy. He spends his time with disciples and followers who don't really understand his mission. He is not in a hurry. He moves through his life with resilience. He does not see setbacks, misunderstanding, or even hatred as the final word. He is rooted in kingdom life so the fruit of his life feeds and redeems the whole world.

In the Garden of Gethsemane, before he was about to be crucified, Jesus asks the Father if it is possible to let the cup of judgment pass him by. Jesus asks liberally. He knows that the Father is good. He knocks. He seeks, but he does not receive the yes of the Father. Instead, he goes to the cross. He endures torture, pain, humiliation, alienation, and death. Jesus asks, and the scandal of the cross is that it is we who receive his salvation. We get the Father's yes.

> **JESUS ASKS LIBERALLY. HE KNOWS THAT THE FATHER IS GOOD. HE KNOCKS. HE SEEKS, BUT HE DOES NOT RECEIVE THE YES OF THE FATHER.**

- How do you react to the reality that Jesus' prayer in the Garden of Gethsemane was answered with silence?

- Tim Keller was fond of saying that Jesus' receiving of the Father's silence means we will always get his yes. How does this affect you as you approach God in prayer?

Jesus' death on the cross is a great exchange: we get his goodness and righteousness credited to our account and he takes on our sin and shame. It is also a victory cry, which widens and dramatizes the frame into one motif called *Christus Victor*. As Fleming Rutledge writes in her book *The Crucifixion*, on the cross and through his struggle in Gethsemane, "The Son of God is about to initiate the decisive battle against the Powers of Darkness." On the cross, Jesus is engaged in a cosmic struggle against the forces of evil. He asks and takes on the wrath of God, not only paying for our individual sins but also confronting the powers and principalities of systems and injustice that strike at our communities and our earth. Salvation is much more than a get-out-of-hell card.

- If Jesus has not only conquered death but has also accomplished the reign of God in the cosmological order, how might this affect the way you approach God in prayer? We can be so timid and inward-focused in our prayers. How might this change for you?

PRACTICE

Take some time in silence and prayer today to ponder Jesus as substitution and as *Christus Victor*. Practice asking, seeking, and knocking, knowing Jesus' life and death defeat the powers of sin and darkness. Where have you seen such evil powers at work in you, your community, or in larger institutions and structures? Pray against the effectiveness of these demonic powers.

WEEK 7

BEARING FRUIT FOR THE SAKE OF OTHERS

MATTHEW 7:12-20

GROUP SESSION

BEGIN

- **Start** with two minutes of silence.
- **Pray** and invite the Spirit to be present, shaping you as people as you discuss.
- **Opening Question:** Given what we've studied so far about fruitfulness, I'm beginning to realize . . .

READ

- **Read Matthew 7:12-20**

WATCH

- **Watch** video

DISCUSS

1. Are you prone to go with the flow in your spiritual life? What are some ways this plays out in your life?
2. Do you tend to be impressed by big numbers or external appearances? Have you encountered a Christian leader who has "fallen from grace"? What did you learn from that experience?
3. What is your reaction to the distinction between growth and health?
4. What activities or attitudes do you think are necessary for healthy spiritual fruit?
5. What have you read so far in Jesus' sermon that you can point to as part of healthy soil or even something necessary about pruning character?
6. What would bearing healthy fruit look like in your life?
7. This week we will think about setting the stage for bearing healthy fruit. To start, how can you begin to develop discernment about the content you consume (whether it's explicitly

Christian or not)? Are there sources you should take a step back from? Are there places you should prioritize?

8. Read Psalm 1, another portion of Scripture that uses agricultural analogies to talk about a fruitful life. Give some examples of what it would look like for you to plant yourself in healthy soil.

CLOSE

- **Remember** that Jesus takes the pressure off.
- **Pray** in small groups. Choose a portion of Psalm 1 or Matthew 7:12-20 to focus your attention on as you pray.

DAY 1 SPIRITUAL IMAGINATION

READ AND REFLECT

- **Start** with two minutes of silence.
- **Read Matthew 7:12.**

Often the task of following Jesus and growing in our faith can feel overwhelming. The Bible is a long book, and there are more long books explaining the Bible! Perhaps we think we need an expert to explain it all to us.

Matthew 7:12 is often called the Golden Rule because it simplifies so much of the complexity of following Jesus. How would you like to be treated when you're feeling stressed, you've made a mistake, or you've overreacted? We'd all like to receive grace in these and other situations, so we should offer grace to others.

- According to the passage, how often and thoroughly must we follow the Golden Rule?

- How might this sort of fruit begin to grow in us?

- **Read Galatians 5:14 and Romans 13:8.** Each are part of Paul's letters to churches. What is Paul saying in each? Is Paul saying the same thing as Matthew 7:12?

- Professor Jonathan Pennington notes that these verses in Matthew are more than a rule and include embodying practical wisdom, character, and flourishing. How does this vision for human fruitfulness summed up in verse 12 help guide your understanding of what a fruitful Christian life looks like? List some of your thoughts below.

In the Golden Rule, Jesus is talking about developing a gospel imagination. We can imagine our way into someone else's shoes, then imagine what it would look like for that person to receive love and act accordingly.

It's more difficult to put the Golden Rule into practice when we're under stress, when resources are tight, or in relation to someone we struggle with. Developing a fruitful life begins with gospel intentionality, imagining ourselves into difficult situations in advance, praying for the Spirit to grow love of others within us, and then putting those prayers and intentions into practice when the moment arises.

PRACTICE

WRITE DOWN three people or situations you can anticipate struggling with. Then spend a few moments praying, and ask the Holy Spirit to guide your imagination. Perhaps you think of a recent interaction with them, or the way your body feels when you say their name, and then bring that to God in prayer3.

Next, write a brief paragraph about each of these people or situations. What would it look like to treat others the way you want to be treated in each of these circumstances?

Conclude by praying that God would be present with you, enabling you to put your gospel imagination into practice.

DAY 2 GOSPEL DISCERNMENT

READ AND REFLECT

- **Start** with two minutes of silence.
- **Read Matthew** 7:13-14.

Jesus' words in these verses are likely to strike modern readers as very, well, *narrow*. It's helpful to understand them in the context of the Sermon on the Mount as a whole. Throughout this study we have seen that it is Jesus' desire for his followers to live fruitful lives. As modern people, we tend to separate knowledge from action, believing that our spiritual lives are simply a matter of what we know. Thus, we are inclined to think that growth in our relationship with God is a matter of acquiring more knowledge about him. There's no doubt that growth will entail learning, but it also involves our *behavior*. Fruitfulness is about transformation, not just information. Using the table titled Two Paths, briefly note the contrast in these few verses. What characterizes these two paths Jesus describes?

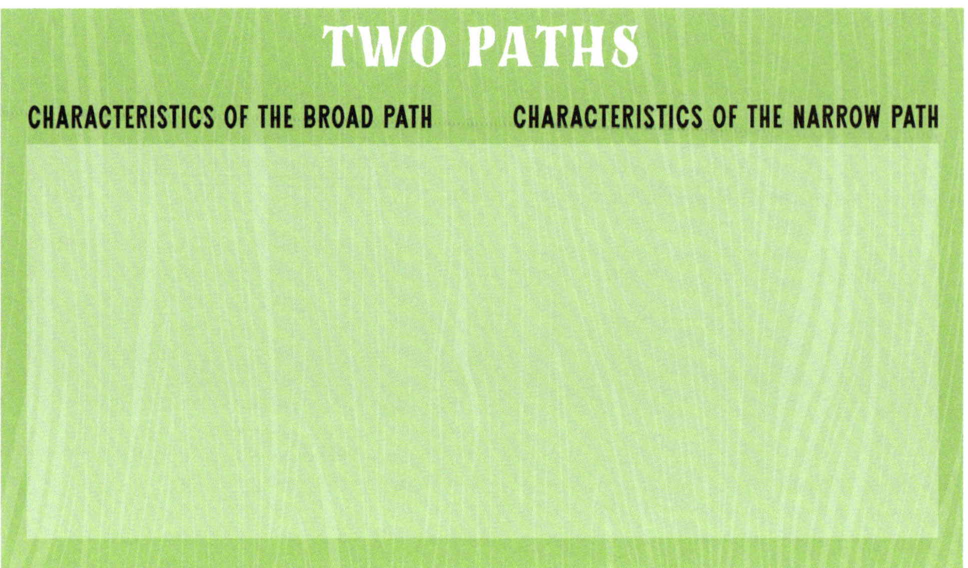

FRUITFULNESS IS ABOUT TRANSFORMATION, NOT JUST INFORMATION.

When Jesus talks about entering "by the narrow gate," he is talking about a way of living. We've seen through our study that this way of life involves a total reorientation of our lives around God and his kingdom. We've seen that this way of life involves an inclination to show mercy to others; it involves daily dependence on God who knows and loves us. It involves entering into a community of loving prayer. It is a life of joyful obedience that bears fruit because we are connected to the One who is the source of life.

- **Read Matthew 7:13-14** again. It's tempting to think we need to do a lot and know a lot or be perfect in our actions to follow Jesus. What do you think is required to find this narrow gate and stay on the narrow path?

- Now READ JOHN 10:9. *Who* is the door? What does this tell us about how we get onto the narrow path and how we stay there?

Practically living in communion with God also requires discernment and focus and a community of fellow disciples who encourage one another along the way. Spiritual growth is not a DIY, solo backpacking trip.

- Use the space below to prayerfully reflect on the areas of your life that help and hinder your journey in this way of life.

- Then think about someone—perhaps someone from the group or another friend—with whom you can share your reflections so that you might better encourage one another in a life of fruitfulness. Write down their name.

PRACTICE

Some areas of our lives may not be characterized by sin but are still hindrances to living a life of joyful obedience to Jesus. These parts of our lives may take up too large a place in our lives, choking out our best intentions. These may be things like the media we consume, the food or beverages we look to for comfort, or the trivialities we use to blow off steam. These hindrances may be fine in moderation, but we should place thoughtful limits around them to ensure that they don't become distractions.

Using the image of a pasture below, write about the hindrances in your life, and the limits you'd like to place on them. Where do you need to place good fences around struggling places so things can grow?

The prompts below are meant to stimulate your thinking about what and to where you tend to go when life becomes challenging:

- Comfort: When I'm feeling bored or anxious I tend to turn to . . .
- Time: I find I do/don't have time for rest or restoration . . .
- Vocation: In my calling and work, I feel the best when . . .
- Vocation: I find I over- or under-function in these circumstances . . .
- Relationships: When I encounter silence or frustration, I . . .

Tomorrow we'll continue this exercise in gospel discernment. For now, finish this time in prayer, thanking God that he is at work in your life!

DAY 3 GOING DEEPER

READ AND REFLECT

- **Start** with two minutes of silence.
- **Read Matthew 7:13-14.**

Today we'll continue yesterday's practice in gospel discernment, thinking about aspects of our lives that help and hinder our spiritual growth. Jesus invites us to "enter by the narrow gate" into a life of bearing fruit as we remain connected to him. Continue to reflect on your life, prayerfully asking God to guide you.

Reread John 10:7. As you read these verses, does Jesus believe that his teachings and he himself are the exclusive way to life?

- In the original Greek language of the verses in Matthew, the final verb is in present tense: "how few *are finding* this way." How does this verb tense reinforce the process of fruitful growth in a disciple's life?

- What might it look like to "enter by the narrow gate" daily? Write down some ideas.

Read Matthew 7:15-20. This passage also deals with true and false prophets. When Jesus talks about knowing someone by their fruits, it's about character built over time.

- As you read verses 15-20, what are Jesus' expectations about false teachers? Given what we've studied so far, write out a few characteristics of false teachers on the one hand and true teachers on the other.

- What is the judgment for false teachers? What is the reminder to Jesus' followers here in light of Jesus' focus on false teachers?

PRACTICE

Yesterday we considered the hindrances in our lives that need to be limited so as not to choke out gospel fruit. Now we consider the areas of our lives that are rebellious and sinful and should be put to death. Repentance is an ongoing part of a fruitful life, in which we honestly come before God and ask him to prune the parts of our lives that do not bear fruit. This isn't the same as the cutting down and being thrown into the fire of verse 19! *Repentance* is a military term that means "about-face." When we repent we stay connected to Jesus, are honest about our failures and motivations, and change course.

WHEN WE REPENT WE STAY CONNECTED TO JESUS, ARE HONEST ABOUT OUR FAILURES AND MOTIVATIONS, AND CHANGE COURSE.

- In the space below, write a prayer of repentance, asking God in his kindness to forgive your sin and prune you so that you may bear fruit.

Here is a starting point:

Lord Christ, as I consider what I turn to that can choke out real life, I bring the following things before you . . .

I realize that growing as a disciple means a daily action of both pruning and adding healthy ingredients to my life and patterns . . .

Another aspect to a life of following Jesus is adding new practices that will help you bear fruit. A gardener adds fertilizer to provide nutrients that are not inherently in the soil, and in the same way disciples journeying along that path of life will occasionally want to add new spiritual practices to their lives, praying that God will use them to bear more fruit.

- In the space below, list one practice that you've done throughout these weeks that you'd like to continue to practice.

Finally, remember that the spiritual journey is not lived alone.

- Once you have spent time prayerfully reflecting on and journaling about the hindrances and sin in your life, and the fertilizer of new practices you'd like to add, use the following prompts about what you'd like to share with your community of fellow disciples:
    - When I long to turn to _______ for comfort, instead I'll practice . . . .
    - I've seen gospel fruit in _____'s life and here is what I notice . . .
    - As I think about companions in this journey, I immediately think of . . .
    - Knowing the Holy Spirit is the one who grows fruit and helps me look more like Jesus, I am . . .

DAY 4 FRUITFULNESS CONNECT THE DOTS

READ AND REFLECT

- START with two minutes of silence.
- READ MATTHEW 7:13-14.

We often think about being a "good Christian" in terms of success. And we often view success in terms of something we can measure. So a successful pastor is measured by the size of the church. A successful Christian might be measured by conversions, or her Bible knowledge, or his hours given in acts of mercy. When we change the metric to fruitfulness, it can be a challenging shift. We can't often measure the slow work of being transformed by the Spirit to look more like Jesus.

To help us connect some dots, think of a Christian you know who you would describe as fruitful. She evidences the fruit of the Spirit. He's unruffled by challenging circumstances. Suffering tends to increase both her vulnerability and her trust in Christ.

WRITE the name of someone you know personally (not someone with whom you're simply mildly acquainted) below. You might want to interview this person as part of your work this week. In the space that follows, write down your responses to the questions below.

- What would you say characterizes that person? What is their fruit?

- What do their emotional reactions look like?

- How do they react when stressed, angry, or disappointed?

- What habits of Christian faithfulness do you know they practice?

- What hardships have they endured that have been transformed for their good and God's glory?

- What keeps them on the narrow way?

- What is it about this person that is attractive to you?

Considering some of the spiritual practices you've tried (such as fasting, lectio divina, different prayer practices, generosity, silence, etc.), what plan can you make to continue with one of them?

PRACTICE

THINK of a TV show you've watched recently or a book you've read. Pay close attention to the fruit of a particular character. How would you answer some of the questions above in the interactions you observed? What motivates him? To where does she run for comfort?

How would you characterize the fruit of his or her life?

WRITE DOWN if there is an instance or example in your reading/viewing of this fruit being shown for what it is. (For example, a persistent habit of gossip leads to the fruit of loneliness.)

CONSIDER sharing about either the character or a fruitful Christian with someone in your family or group sometime this week. In this time, discuss together what a model of fruitfulness versus "success" or performance would do in the communities of which you are a part.

DAY 5 JESUS IS THE GATE

READ AND REFLECT

→ **START** with two minutes of silence.

Each week during the Day 5 lesson, we will spend some time meditating on the ways Jesus implements his teaching from the Sermon on the Mount and shows us what a fruitful life looks like.

→ **READ MATTHEW 7:12-20.**

In this portion of the Sermon on the Mount, we've seen that following Jesus is not simply about acquiring more information about God and his Word but about a transformed life that bears fruit. This is a way of life, Jesus tells us, that must be entered in a particular way, through a gate that not many will find. Living this way of life will require the discernment and intention of Jesus' disciples, and a willingness to swim against the current of prevailing culture.

Yet it would be easy to conclude that the way we live the Christian life means clenching our fists and gritting our teeth. A lot of Christians reach this conclusion, but it's important to understand how Jesus' life, death, and resurrection transform our motivation for obedience.

- **READ JOHN 10:7-10**, a passage where Jesus likens his people to sheep. What similarities do you notice between the passage in John and Matthew 7:12-20?

John 10 helps us to see that the "gate" by which we enter that narrow way that leads to life is Jesus himself. We are not called to look for a mysterious entrance—perhaps found through secret knowledge, a technique that will put us on the right path, or even a pile of behaviors to earn gold stars.

- In this passage in John, where does the gate lead? If we think about this metaphor in terms of fruitfulness, what types of trees is Jesus growing in this safe place?

- **Read John 10:3-4.** What characterizes the shepherd, Jesus?

Jesus leads and guides his followers, tenderly caring for us on the path of life. When we don't know which way to go, we can run to him. When we get tired, when we stumble and fail—and we will!—we can trust that he will pick us up and carry us.

Ultimately, we can take comfort knowing that Jesus has already lived the fruitful life. It didn't look the way anyone would have expected. He was constantly swimming against the current. But in doing so, he demonstrated what a life oriented around God looks like.

As Jesus goes to the cross, he transfers his perfection to his followers, giving us his record and taking our sin in exchange. We are therefore free in Christ to live life in the way he calls us to, not grinding out a life of burdensome obedience but freely and lightly pursuing the path he lays before us. God's law becomes the guardrails that do more than simply restrain evil or convict us; the law then becomes a joyful path toward real, flourishing life. Jesus reminds us that he came to fulfill (literally to fill it full) the law.

Because Jesus is the good shepherd by whom we enter the path to life, and because he leads us in this life of fruitfulness that he already lived and credited to us, we can seek after this way of life with intention, motivated by the joy of knowing him.

PRACTICE

- **Prayerfully reflect on your motivation for following Jesus on the path of life. Do you believe it is good to follow him? Do you believe following Jesus is the better way?**

In *The Message*, Eugene Peterson writes of following Jesus (in his paraphrase of Matthew 11:28-30): "Are you tired? Worn out? Burned out on religion? Come to me. Get away with me and you'll recover your life. I'll show you how to take a real rest. Walk with me and work with me—watch how I do it. Learn the unforced rhythms of grace. I won't lay anything heavy or ill-fitting on you. Keep company with me and you'll learn to live freely and lightly."

- **Underline or circle words in this passage that stand out to you. Then write them in the space below. Are there patterns that you notice in the words you chose? Do they speak to something that needs to change or a desire for union with Christ? Write any thoughts below.**

Spend some time in prayer: reflect back to God your gratitude for Jesus, the good shepherd who opens the door to his sheep and leads us in the path of life.

WEEK 8

BEARING FRUIT TO THE END

MATTHEW 7:21-29

GROUP SESSION

BEGIN

- **Start** with two minutes of silence.
- **Pray** and invite the Spirit to be present, shaping you as people as you discuss.
- **Opening Question:** As you've worked through the Sermon on the Mount, what is one takeaway for you?

READ

- **Read Matthew 7:21-29.**

WATCH

- **Watch** video

DISCUSS

1. Reading Matthew 7:21-23, what is the difference between those who are and those who aren't in God's kingdom?
2. Does this end to Jesus' sermon surprise you? Why or why not?
3. How have you seen how God's law can be used to restrain evil in society?
4. Discuss the ways in which God's law has brought you to your own need for a Savior. Is there a particular part of the Sermon on the Mount that has felt pointed for you during this study?
5. What is Jesus' attitude toward doing things for God (see verses 22 and 24)? What's the contrast between these people who do things for God?
6. How might we actually do the things the Sermon on the Mount asks of us?
7. Is there a time in your life when being confronted by your own sin led to concrete action?
8. Frederick Dale Bruner writes about this life of discipleship as exercise: "The summons to our knees is never an end in itself; the calisthenic of this sermon is to move repeatedly from

kneeling to walking. The direction of the Sermon on the Mount is *to* the deed—but it is equally *from* the gift. It is *toward* the neighbor *through* the Father." Given the Bruner quote about the "calisthenics" of the sermon, where are you weak? What movement needs strengthening?

9. What is one thing you want to pray and act on for guidance concerning loving God and loving your neighbor?

10. Is there something as an individual or group that you want to continue to practice or commit to given this study?

CLOSE

→ **Remember** that Jesus takes the pressure off.

→ **Pray** in smaller groups of two or three. Bring your opening takeaway or your answer to the question of "calisthenics" to prayer.

DAY 1 WHAT DO WE DO?

READ AND REFLECT

- **Start** with two minutes of silence.
- **Read Matthew 7:21-23.**

Read the passage slowly a few times:

> Not everyone who says to me, "Lord, Lord," will enter the kingdom of heaven, but the one who does the will of my Father who is in heaven. On that day many will say to me, "Lord, Lord, did we not prophesy in your name, and cast out demons in your name, and do many mighty works in your name?" And then will I declare to them, "I never knew you; depart from me, you workers of lawlessness."

- According to this passage, what is the mark of true, saving faith?

Here, religious teachers did many spectacular things—including exorcism and prophecy!—isn't that fruit? But, they aren't known by Jesus. At the same time, the wise builder actually does what God requires. When we read these verses along with the following verses on the wise and foolish builder it seems confusing—Which is it? Is it what we do or not do that will be a deciding factor about entering the kingdom of heaven?

The key to understanding is that when these religious people want to be part of God's kingdom, they choose to use their religious works as an entrance fee. These, they think, should warrant God's kingdom.

- What seems to be the key about entrance into the kingdom of heaven?

- Go back to the Beatitudes in Matthew 5. What, again, characterizes those who enter the kingdom? How are these teachers different?

- Jesus talks about not *knowing* these spectacular teachers. Despite all their "Christian" work, they did not know Christ. What does it mean to know Christ and to have him know you? Write an answer in your own words.

There are many types of knowing: some is gained through the acquisition of knowledge or practice, some of it accrues over a lifetime of intimate knowledge. Some knowing is bodily or musical, some is intuitive, and some is practiced and learned. We know a best friend differently than we know an influencer on social media. We may feel like we know the influencer, but we are completely unknown to them.

- How might this help you think about knowing Jesus and being known by him?

PRACTICE

- Today, in your minutes of silence and prayer consider: Was there a word or phrase that stuck out to you in your reading?

What have you learned about Jesus as you've studied the Sermon on the Mount? Is there a way in which you need to bring that knowledge home to yourself and start an honest conversation with God about it? Spend as much time as you like, but try to spend at least ten minutes speaking and listening to God concerning this passage and your desire to be known by Jesus.

DAY 2 DISCIPLES OF JESUS

READ AND REFLECT

- **Start** with two minutes of silence.
- **Read Matthew 7:21-29.**

Throughout Matthew chapter 7, Jesus sets up contrasting pairs: the wise and foolish builder, the true and false disciples and prophets, and the narrow and wide gates. Each is meant to show us the path of discipleship.

As we've seen throughout the study, discipleship (or apprenticeship) to Jesus is the process by which we enter through the narrow gate of Christ himself and, through the Spirit, are empowered to live our ordinary lives following Jesus. Discipleship isn't about prominence or visibility, but it is about faithfulness and fruitfulness.

Everything—from our money to our emotions, our generosity and prayer—is under the lordship of Jesus. And how we relate to God and others is seen by all: we are known by our life's fruit.

We cannot be Christians in name only; to be a Christian is to be a disciple and follower of Jesus. We've spoken throughout this study that fruitfulness means living and loving like Jesus. This comes from Dallas Willard who writes about apprenticeship to Jesus as living as Jesus would live if he were in your place and time with your gifts and life.

- How do you react to this idea?

- In your past, what has being a disciple of Jesus meant? Has it meant extra activities, extra work, or some particular emotional experience?

- From these weeks studying the Sermon on the Mount, write down in your own words what characterizes a disciple of Jesus.

- As we consider the fruitful life, can you point to ways the soil you're in has become more healthy? Or places where you've been pruned so that more fruit can grow? Perhaps you've seen how a fallow season is part of the process, or you've been encouraged by new shoots growing. Write down some thoughts below.

PRACTICE

On the tree image below, take a few minutes in thoughtful prayer and silence to write down what characterizes your life as a disciple. Who do you follow?

- ***Roots:*** What are the hidden things that bring you life? Where do you go when you're weary, sad, joyful, or embarrassed?

- ***Trunk:*** What sorts of foundational habits anchor you (for example, a morning run, Bible reading, late-night TV watching, conversation with a friend)?

- ***Branches:*** In what areas are you paying attention to the leading of Jesus for your life (vocational duties, growth in grace, heart for service or evangelism, a particular character trait or need of your place and community, among others)?

- ***Fruit:*** When someone looks at your life and apprenticeship to Jesus, how would they characterize your actions and heart attitudes? Does it move you into places or roles that are both natural and stretching?

- **WRITE DOWN** any concluding thoughts from this exercise.

DAY 3 TRANSFORMED DISCIPLES

READ AND REFLECT

→ START with two minutes of silence.

Below you'll find some themes in the Sermon on the Mount. Pick one or two points to focus on for your study today.

→ Jesus' invitation: Matthew 5:1, 12-20; 7:28-29

→ Desiring the kingdom: Matthew 5:3-12; 7:13-23

→ Sin and lackluster fruit: Matthew 5:21-30; 6:25-34

→ Judgment and mercy: Matthew 5:38-48; 7:1-6

→ Seeking after God: Matthew 6:9-14; 7:7-12

→ A faithful and fruitful life: Matthew 5:13-16; 7:24-29

After you've read the passages you chose, answer the following:

- What is Jesus asking of his followers? Or, what is he condemning?

- What might this obedience look like in your life?

- How has your time with the grouped passages helped clarify the virtues of a fruitful disciple?

In *The Divine Conspiracy*, Dallas Willard writes, "Kingdom obedience is kingdom abundance." Often we pull these two concepts apart; obedience feels stifling and abundance feels too good to be true. How does obedience get us to the abundant, fruitful life that Jesus says will characterize his followers? We might think that a sudden transformation in circumstances or desires might get us to really love and follow Jesus as he commands.

Yet, Willard also writes, "To believe something is to act as if it is so." In the same way that we are not brains on a stick, and that we realize that our bodies, souls, minds, wills, emotions, circumstances, contexts, and histories all play a part in who we are, so it is with our discipleship to Christ. Jesus is saying that we get to the fruitful life by actually following his teaching in the Sermon on the Mount. To do so, we have to get our whole selves involved.

To be transformed disciples, the practice of delighting in God through the practice of silence, solitude, and stillness can be really helpful.

- **Reflect** on your daily and corporate times of silence and solitude. How has this been a fruitful practice for you? What has it brought up?

> **WE ALSO MUST PRACTICE ACTUALLY OBEYING THE WORDS OF THE SERMON ON THE MOUNT IN OUR BODIES.**

We also must practice actually obeying the words of the Sermon on the Mount in our bodies. If you wanted to make a bodily change for your health, for example, you'd actually need to change your diet and add exercise.

- As you read today, what particularly from the Sermon on the Mount do you want to continue to practice?

- What might it look like to actually intend to do this thing? Write down some practical steps you need to take.

- How will you grow in this area? What will steps of accountability look like? How will you get feedback?

- What is your time frame and your hope and desire surrounding this act of obedience?

PRACTICE

PRAY and spend your time dwelling on Jesus. Bring your act of obedience to him, knowing he cares for you, loves you, desires good for you, and through you blesses your community.

Find a way to make your desires or next steps visual: add it to your calendar, put it on a sticky note on your bathroom mirror, or create a drawing or art to remind you of God's faithfulness. Finally share your action of obedience to Jesus' sermon with someone from your group today.

DAY 4 ON CHRIST, THE SOLID ROCK

READ AND REFLECT

- **Start** with two minutes of silence.
- **Read Matthew 7:24-29.**

- What differentiates the wise and foolish builders in these verses?

- In verses 26-27, how does Jesus extend the analogy to his listeners? Who is foolish or wise?

- What was the reaction of the crowds (v. 29)? What takeaways do you have from exploring these verses?

Edward Mote was the pastor of Rehoboth Baptist Church in West Sussex, England, for twenty-six years in the mid-1800s. He became a preacher only in his fifties. Before that, he trained and worked as a cabinetmaker in London. He's also the author of the hymn, "My Hope Is Built on Nothing Less," which comes from the story of the wise and foolish builders in the Sermon on the Mount.

The lyrics are below:

My hope is built on nothing less
Than Jesus' blood and righteousness.
I dare not trust the sweetest frame
But wholly lean on Jesus' name.

Refrain:

On Christ, the solid rock, I stand;
All other ground is sinking sand,
All other ground is sinking sand.

In every rough and stormy gale,
My anchor holds within the vale.
When all around my soul gives way,
He then is all my hope and stay. [Refrain]

Not earth, nor hell, my soul can move;
I rest upon unchanging love.
I trust his righteous character,
His counsel, promise, and his power. [Refrain]

When he shall come with trumpet sound,
Oh, may I then in Him be found,
Dressed in His righteousness alone,
Faultless to stand before the throne. [Refrain]

- **Circle** the words that stick out to you as you read through this hymn.
- **Read** through the hymn a second time. **Underline** your desires surrounding connection to God as your "solid rock."
- **Put a check mark** next to areas where you sense the Spirit inviting you to repent.

Christ is our "solid rock": our foundation for all of life, no matter its turmoil or suffering. Remember the times when you have experienced Jesus as a rock. Was there something different from how you experience his presence now?

PRACTICE

- In prayer, bring your circled words to Jesus. Tell him how these words help to name your desires and your faith journey.

- Next, bring your underlined words in prayer. Name your desires before your good and kind Father.

- Now, in company with the Spirit, name those areas of where you fall short and need his help.

- As you commune with the triune God through Scripture and the words of the hymn, spend a few minutes finally resting in the presence of Christ. How does he see you? What would it look like to build your life on him in concrete action?

DAY 5 THE ONE WITH AUTHORITY

READ AND REFLECT

➜ **Start** with two minutes of silence.

Each week during the Day 5 lesson, we will spend some time meditating on the ways Jesus implements his teaching from the Sermon on the Mount and shows us what a fruitful life looks like.

➜ **Read Matthew** *7:28-29.*

Read Mark 10:17-27, an instance where Jesus' way confronts a young man's dreams.

- What is the rich young ruler's response to Jesus' call?

- How do Jesus' disciples respond to the ruler's reaction?

- What words of assurance does Jesus offer?

Read Matthew 7:28-29 again. Here, the response to Jesus' sermon is amazement at Jesus' authority. Jesus is not just a wise and intelligent teacher, he is the One who says: "If you've seen me, you've seen the Father" (see John 14:9). Jesus is the preexistent second person of the Trinity who holds all authority.

- How do you react to the word *authority*? What characterizes loving and powerful authority?

- What is your response to Jesus given your study of his Sermon?

Matthew Henry writes in his commentary in the early 1700s: "Christ, upon the mountain, showed more true authority, than the scribes in Moses' seat. Thus when Christ teaches by his Spirit in the soul, he teaches with authority. He says, *Let there be light, and there is light.*" The God who commands something to come into being, light, is the same God delivering the Sermon on the Mount. God is able to effect the change that the law of God requires. He is the One with authority.

> **GOD IS ABLE TO EFFECT THE CHANGE THAT THE LAW OF GOD REQUIRES.**

- What is your understanding of the word *authority* as it relates to Jesus? What does it imply and how does Jesus demand it and receive it?

- If Jesus has all authority, who grows fruit in disciples?

- Does this help you step into joyful obedience, knowing that fruitfulness is both part of your agency and not up to you?

- What action steps are you taking that you've seen the Spirit use to grow fruit in you over the course of this study?

- What do you want to ask Jesus for in response?

PRACTICE

- **The house of our lives will stand or fall based on the foundation the house has been built upon. Spend some time flipping through and reviewing the pages of this study. What is a good next step for you and your community?**

NOW WHAT?

After weeks of studying the Sermon on the Mount, you're likely left with both the goodness of Jesus and the enormity of the task of living as a disciple. It can feel life changing, promising, *and* overwhelming! You might be asking, now what?

Dallas Willard spoke of spiritual transformation as a "golden triangle" involving three points: (1) the action of the Holy Spirit, (2) the planned discipline to put on a new heart, and (3) the ordinary events and temptations of life.

But how will we grow and change? It isn't by waiting for a perfect time or being zapped into a deeper spirituality, and it definitely doesn't require an ecstatic moment. Instead, we become fruitful Christian disciples through a combination of listening to our life and temptations, centering our mind on Christ, practicing spiritual habits, and praying for the movement of the Spirit.

We all will experience hardship, suffering, and pain. The house of our lives will stand or fall based on the foundation the house has been built upon. Transformation happens by the mysterious work of the Spirit through circumstances we can't control. What we *can* control is our own planned discipline to put on a new heart. We must *do* something to grow.

In our church, we end each service with a benediction, a good word, to send us out into the world with the blessing of our Father, the fellowship we enjoy in the Spirit, through the saving work of the Son. We respond collectively: "He is Lord indeed! Let us go forth to serve the world as those who love our Lord and Savior Jesus Christ!" That is, we're invited to go out and *do* something because we've experienced the love and grace offered to us in Jesus.

So, as you move on from this study, what will you go and do?

You are invited to be what psychiatrist and author Curt Thompson often speaks about—to *become* the Sermon on the Mount. We're not simply people who do the things mentioned in it as if we were checking off boxes, but we become an embodied form of the sermon.

May you be blessed to be a blessing.

APPENDIX

A NOTE ON SILENCE

THROUGHOUT THESE WEEKS as we study the Sermon on the Mount, we will be practicing both individual and corporate times of silence. As this practice is new for many believers, we want to do our best to welcome you into this practice.

Silence helps us remember in our bodies that the point of being Jesus' disciple isn't about what we achieve or say, but through the practice of silence, we become aware of Christ at work in us. Silence untethers us from getting our worth from what we do and produce. Since what we say and do is formed by who we are, silence in the presence of God helps to form us.

Practicing silence is not akin to emptying your mind as in Eastern practices of meditation. It isn't prayer time either. It is a practice of slowing your body, mind, and soul to experience the reality and presence of God in a real time and real place. In the same way that you need time together with a friend, we need unhurried time with God.

THE BENEFITS OF SILENCE

Silence opens us up to actually experience the "still small voice" of God. Silence can help quiet our minds and bodies to hear God.

In his devotional book *Emotionally Healthy Spirituality Day by Day*, Pete Scazzero writes about silence in connection to emotional health. The goal of silence is to "cultivate our personal relationship with him—to be with God—surrendering our will to his will, our presence to his presence, and our actions to his actions each day." Thus, "silence and stillness with God are a foundational practice by which we actually position ourselves for God to do his transformative work in us." While many mainstream practices promote silence as a way to achieve peace, choosing to practice silence before God is more than just getting a sense of calm. It is a process by which we open ourselves up to God's work in us.

Silence trains us to be present in the moment. While we spend much of our thinking time in the past or the future, the present moment is all we have as a space for actual attention to God and connecting to oneself and others. Because silence can feel awkward, we tend to avoid it as much as possible. In doing so, we distract ourselves instead of recognizing God's presence with us.

In his book *The Soul of Shame*, Christian author and psychiatrist Curt Thompson writes about the vulnerability necessary for silence, and the deep healing God brings with it:

> We deeply long for connection, to be seen and known for who we are without rejection. But we are terrified of the vulnerability that is required for that very contact. And shame is the variable that mediates that fear of rejection in the face of vulnerability.
>
> But in the Trinity we see something that we must pay attention to: God does not leave. The loving relationship shared between Father, Son and Spirit is the ground on which all other models of life and creativity rest. In this relationship of constant self-giving, vulnerable and joyful love, shame has no oxygen to breathe.

Silence is about learning to simply be with God, the One who will not leave us.

HOW DO I START?

Some practical starting places: When you start practicing silence, use a timer for your two minutes. You may want to increase the time as you move along. Be comfortable and close your eyes. Give your time to God; you may want to say a line from the Bible or a reminder before you enter your time of silence. ("I commit this time to you, Abba Father," "I am yours," or "Your yoke is easy," are all good starting points.)

It's likely that as you begin to practice silence, you'll find your mind flooded with all sorts of thoughts—you'll start making a to-do list or remember what you need to communicate to someone—when you stop and slow down. This is normal. Simply offer those thoughts to God and return to a word, such as "Jesus," to get you back into a receptive posture. As you practice silence, you may hear the voice of God nudging you, you may be presented with an image in your mind, or you may gain clarity. Practicing silence isn't about a spiritual experience to get something from God. It is a time to simply be his child, delighting in his presence.

Silence may feel strange or uncomfortable at first, and that's okay. Most new practices take some time for adjustment. We encourage you to give it a try and to stick with it. We live in a world that is obsessed with busyness and tells us that we find our value in what we produce. Silence is a countercultural practice that weans us from efficiency and productivity as our highest good and helps us reorient our lives around God himself. We encourage you to give yourself grace as you begin this journey, looking with hope to God who invites you into a life of fruitfulness.

SUGGESTIONS FOR FURTHER STUDY AND WORKS REFERENCED

Frederick Dale Bruner, *Matthew: The Christbook*, vol. 1, *Matthew 1–12*, revised and expanded (Grand Rapids, MI: Eerdmans, 2004).

Andy Crouch, *The Life We're Looking For* (New York: Convergent, 2022).

Jonathan Eig, *King: A Life* (New York: Farrar, Straus and Giroux, 2023).

Steven Garber, *A Seamless Life* (Downers Grove, IL: InterVarsity Press, 2023) and *Visions of Vocation* (Downers Grove, IL: InterVarsity Press, 2014).

Matthew Henry, *Matthew Henry's Complete Bible Commentary* (Peabody, MA: Hendrickson, 2008).

Timothy Keller, *Generous Justice* (New York: Dutton, 2010) and *The Prodigal God* (Grand Rapids, MI: Zondervan, 2009).

Anne Lamott, *Help, Thanks, Wow: The Three Essential Prayers* (New York: Riverhead, 2012).

Martin Luther King Jr., "Love Your Enemies" (sermon at Dexter Avenue Baptist Church in Montgomery, Alabama, November 17, 1957).

Martyn Lloyd-Jones, *Studies in the Sermon on the Mount* (Grand Rapids, MI: Eerdmans, 1971).

Robert Murray M'Cheyne, *Sermons of Murray M'Cheyne* (London: Banner of Truth Trust, 1971).

Jonathan Pennington, *The Sermon on the Mount and Human Flourishing: A Theological Commentary* (Grand Rapids, MI: Baker Academic, 2017).

Eugene Peterson, *The Message: The Bible in Contemporary Language* (Colorado Springs: NavPress, 2005) and *A Long Obedience in the Same Direction: Discipleship in an Instant Society,* commemorative ed. (Downers Grove, IL: InterVarsity Press, 2024).

Fleming Rutledge, *Advent: The Once and Future Coming of Jesus Christ* (Grand Rapids, MI: Eerdmans, 2018) and *The Crucifixion: Understanding the Death of Jesus Christ* (Grand Rapids, MI: Eerdmans, 2015).

John Stott, *The Message of the Sermon on the Mount,* rev. ed. (Downers Grove, IL: IVP Academic, 2020).

Curt Thompson, *The Soul of Shame* (Downers Grove, IL: InterVarsity, 2015).

Dallas Willard, *The Divine Conspiracy: Rediscovering Our Hidden Life in God* (San Francisco: Harper SanFrancisco, 1998), *The Spirit of the Disciplines* (San Francisco: HarperSanFrancisco, 1988), and *The Great Omission* (San Francisco: HarperSanFrancisco, 2006).

ALSO BY ASHLEY HALES

ASHLEY HALES (PhD, University of Edinburgh) is editorial director for print at *Christianity Today*. She is the author of *Finding Holy in the Suburbs* and *A Spacious Life*, and her work focuses on the surprising and renewing work of a Christian imagination. She is a Kirby Laing Centre academic fellow, an advisor to the Covenant College board of trustees, and a cofounder of The Willowbrae Institute. Ashley lives on the central coast of California with her husband, Bryce, and their four children.

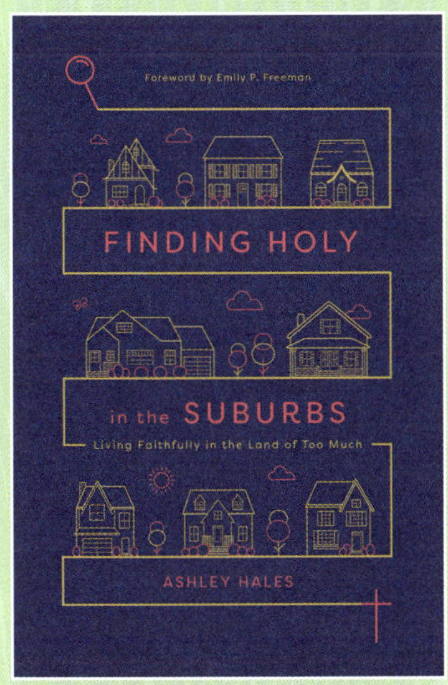

Finding Holy in the Suburbs
978-0-8308-4545-3

A Spacious Life
978-0-8308-4738-9

TRANSFORM YOUR BIBLE STUDY EXPERIENCE WITH INTERVARSITY PRESS

These Bible studies offer you a fresh opportunity to engage with Scripture. Each study includes:

- weekly sessions for a group of any size
- access to weekly teaching videos
- five days of individual study and reflection each week

The refreshing, accessible, and insightful content from trusted Bible teachers will encourage you in your faith!

With guidance from trusted Bible teachers, this collection of Bible studies invites groups and individuals to take a closer look at Scripture and offers practices that create space for prayer and worship, lament, and wonder.

Each six- to eight-week study explores Scripture through a thematic lens, beginning each week with a group session that includes both video teaching and discussion questions, followed by five days of individual study and reflection.

Like this book?

Scan the code to discover more content like this!

Get on IVP's email list to receive special offers, exclusive book news, and thoughtful content from your favorite authors on topics you care about.

IVPRESS.COM/BOOK-QR